Change For Children

Authors

Sandra Nina Kaplan
Jo Ann Butom Kaplan
Sheila Kunishima Madsen
Bette K. Taylor

Goodyear Publishing Company, Inc.
Pacific Palisades, California

Change For Children

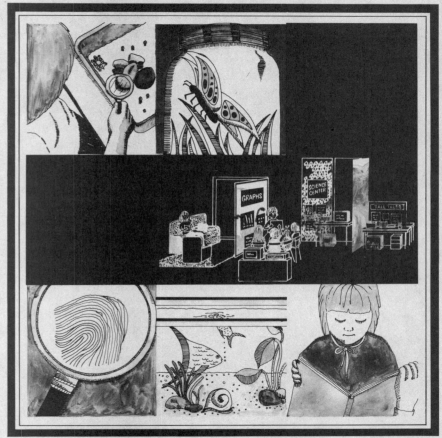

Ideas and Activities for Individualizing Learning

Copyright © 1973
GOODYEAR PUBLISHING COMPANY, INC.
Pacific Palisades, California

Current printing (last digit):
10 9 8 7
ISBN: 0-87620-145-1

Library of Congress Catalog
Card Number: 72-94423

Y-1451-7

Printed in the United States of America

For ALL the students in Inglewood
who helped make our ideas work.

Goodyear Education Series

Theodore W. Hipple, Editor
University of Florida

Contents

Preface

WHY THIS BOOK

Why educational methods of instruction have to change has been ably explained in current literature and research by noted educators. *How* these changes can be implemented in the classroom is the "now" problem for teachers. "We know where we want to go, but we don't know how to get there," is the statement frequently heard among teachers. This expectation for change creates a need for some guide or model so that this change can occur.

The activities and techniques presented in this book provide a guide and model for teachers to individualize learning within their classrooms. They provide a step-by-step approach to changing the classroom environment, developing and placing learning activities in the room, and devising plans and schedules of student and teacher time. In addition, guides are presented for developing an independent study program. Ideas for record keeping and evaluation complete the total program of individualizing learning.

These activities are not intended to put teachers into a mold, but rather to help them create their own individualized learning program. Teachers may choose those parts of the book which are most appropriate for their student and teacher needs and interests.

Many of the techniques for individualizing learning have been presented in a step-by-step format. However, not all the steps may be used by all children. The individual differences of children will determine which steps they will use and the order in which they will use them.

The success we had in initiating an individualized learning program was based on the ideas and techniques presented in this book. After working with teachers and hearing their pleas for concrete methods to help them begin programs of their own, we decided to make our ideas available. We hope that the following pages will be an aid to teachers who want to make the transition from knowing about individualized learning to practicing individualized learning.

Introduction

DEFINING INDIVIDUALIZED LEARNING

Personalized Instruction   Open Structure
Stylized Learning   Individualized Instruction
Humanized Education   Custom-tailored Learning

Educators have coined many terms to describe what they mean by individualized learning. As it applies to the ideas and techniques presented in this book, individualized learning is the process of developing and retaining *individuality* by a classroom organization that provides for the effective and efficient learning experiences of *each* class member. Teaching and learning methods which focus on the total class are replaced by those which cater to individual differences. The need to label and categorize students in order to attend to their differences is lessened when each class member is attended to as an individual. Individualized learning comes about by varying the teaching and learning processes according to the interests, preferences, sociometrics, learning styles, and abilities and achievements of the students.

Adding the word individualized to learning does not mean that the teacher instructs every child individually, nor does it mean that group instruction is taboo. Grouping students for academic and social learning is a necessary component of an individualized classroom. Learning to interact, cooperate, and work as a group member is vital to the development of each child as an individual. Flexible groups which pull students together for a specific purpose aid the teacher in individualizing learning. Students should be members of various groups in order to have various experiences. The goal is to insure that no child becomes a permanent member of either a high, average, or low group.

THE CHANGE PROCESS

The provision of a wide range of materials and activities to create an indoor/outdoor learning environment.
The appropriateness of activities for different types of students.
The opportunities for students to make decisions about what they learn.
The teacher's interaction with students based on knowledge of the learning process.

These are the benchmarks for assessing whether the teacher has made the transition to an individualized learning classroom.

Rearranging the furniture
Stuffing the room with things
Allowing students to move about the room

These changes do not insure that a teacher is individualizing learning. What is visible in the classroom cannot be used as the measure for determining the effectiveness of the teaching/learning process. The teacher must focus attention on how students learn rather than on the content of the subjects taught. The teacher must become a specialist in relationships: child to child, child to teacher, and child to learning. By interacting with students while promoting learning the teacher becomes the intermediary between the child and his environment. He must question, encourage, conference, and share. In this way, he will help make the environment useful for the student. Although the teacher's age, experience, and training are the basis for his authority in the classroom, he must exercise this authority to make learning available to students rather than to impose it on them.

EXPECTATIONS AND EVALUATION

The number of changes which take place is not important. How fast things change in the process of individualizing learning is not important. What is important is that the teacher can answer these questions for himself:

Why am I doing this?
What do I hope to accomplish by this action?
How do I feel about what will be changed?

Success is determined by the teacher's ability to decide what needs to be changed and how these changes can be implemented. Introspection will determine the teacher's tolerance for student noise, mobility, and decision making in the assessment of how much change is acceptable. The teacher needs to develop a philosophical framework from which he can operate. An understanding of why changes are made substantiates these changes to the students, their parents, and the teacher's colleagues.

"My class was choosing the same activities, turning in sloppy work, and using materials in the same way day after day. I had so much fear of manipulating children and of imposing my standards on them that I did nothing at all. I thought that when the time was right for them they would come to me, or they would discover what they needed for themselves. I just decided that I had a responsibility to step in and provide what they were asking for and what I felt was necessary for them at the time."

Individualizing learning does not imply that the teacher will abdicate the responsibility for making some decisions and directing some learnings for the students. The teacher must decide when and where to function as a group member or group leader. Nor does it mean that the teacher will allow or accept anything students do. The goal of individualized learning is to create new standards for learning and behavior, not to abolish or disregard all standards. As the adult, facilitator, friend, and teacher, he is still accountable for the behavior and performance of his students. Teacher accountability assumes a different dimension in the individualized classroom. Although not accountable for teaching all the students the same body of knowledge and skills, he is accountable for teaching each student how to direct his learning in relationship to his individual learning style and needs. In an individualized learning classroom, the major emphasis in evaluating students is on the processes of learning, not on the products of learning. This does not exclude the fact that in any type of learning environment, the students must learn basic and fundamental skills.

"After two years of trial and error in moving into individualizing, I really thought I was ready for my third year. So I set up the environment, gave children the opportunity to make choices, made a variety of materials and working spaces available, and readied myself for that first day. After a month we were still in an unhappy state of chaos. I had ignored the most important factor: the children—a set of students who had had little experience with making choices and assuming real responsibility at school. They seemed to need support and training in how to make appropriate decisions and carry through on commitments. I realized that they needed to go through the same process that I had gone through: taking small steps and beginning with one area. We set up a decision-making center where all the activities were geared to teach and reinforce the process of decision making. We had lots of class meetings, some with imaginary situations and others with actual happenings in our class. We began some self-scheduling for one time block a day. Slowly, I gave and they accepted and asked for more responsibility."

Students cannot be expected to change just because the classroom environment and the teacher have changed. Not all students will be ready or able to adjust themselves to some or all aspects of an individualized learning classroom. The teacher must exercise judgment in order to determine which students manifest the maturity and skill to function successfully in this type of learning environment. The skills needed to work in an individualized classroom must be taught and practiced in the same way other subject area skills are taught and practiced.

" 'This has been one hell of a week . . . . You name it, it's happened. I'm going back to straight rows and three-group reading.'

This kind of feeling has come up more than once in this process of change I've been going through. At these times I've found it necessary to pull in the reins and set up tighter limits and standards. Somehow, just naturally, I find myself and the class moving out again into a more open situation. These periods of pulling in, at least for me, seem to provide a time for some stability and re-evaluation of what might have been going wrong. In other words a few setbacks don't mean you're a failure. They may help you eventually move further ahead."

The students and teacher try and evaluate, move ahead and step back. This is the process of making the transition to an individualized classroom. Opportunities for the class to share and discuss their frustrations, concerns, failures, and successes are important in making the change process understood and effective.

THE LEARNING CENTER APPROACH
TO INDIVIDUALIZING LEARNING

The development and use of learning centers is only one method for individualizing learning. They provide a beginning point but are not intended to be the only source of individualizing instruction. Learning centers become the vehicles for moving students away from teacher-dominated learning experiences and toward student-selected learning activities. Learning centers organize and direct learning experiences for students by allowing freedom while providing structure.

Room Environment
and Room Organization
1

THE ENVIRONMENT AS THE LEARNING CATALYST

What is placed in the room and how it is arranged determines the atmosphere and the expectancies for learning. Since the room becomes the source for initiating and organizing learning activities, what is included, and its availability to the students is of primary importance. All criteria must apply to giving the students freedom to move, both academically and physically. Every part of the room should have the potential for student experience or discovery of some type of learning. Thus, the room's environment is a resource for promoting social, emotional, and academic growth.

The confines of the classroom represent only one type of environment in which children can learn. The environment outside of the classroom must also be considered as a resource for learning. For students in an individualized program of instruction, the optimum learning environment is one which integrates the classroom with the school, the home, and the community.

ROOM ENVIRONMENT CHECKLIST

CHECK   utilizing space to provide a balance between quiet and noisy work areas

CHECK   providing areas for independent study and group interaction

CHECK   labeling areas and posting directions for using each area

CHECK   providing containers and spaces for making materials available to children

CHECK   creating places to display children's work

CHECK   devising ways to obtain human resources and materials

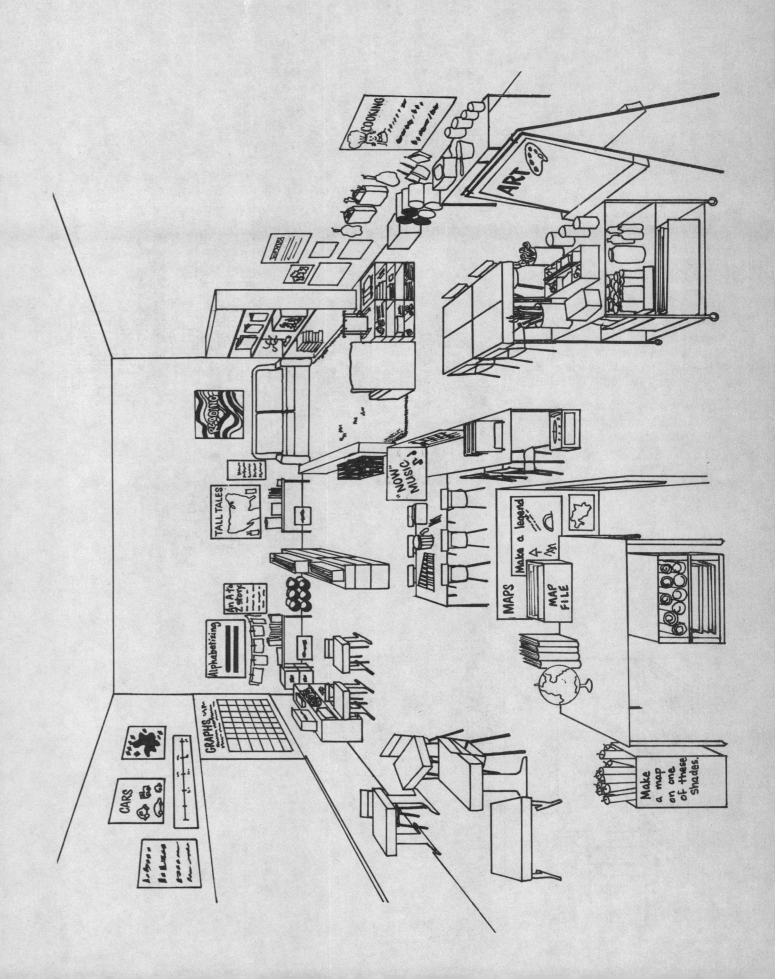

CREATING CLASSROOM SECTIONS TO MEET CHILDREN'S NEEDS

Sectioning parts of the room into learning centers and working areas helps to make more efficient use of classroom space while providing an atmosphere where children can be actively involved in learning. Establishing nooks and crannies within the classroom creates an environment which serves the needs of children: a place to talk, a place to be alone, a place to work with friends, a place to work quietly, a place to be lively, and a place to sit and think.

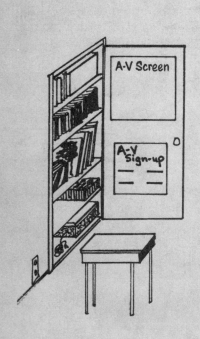

NOOKS AND CRANNIES

Cloth Divider

An artistic and utilitarian room divider can be formed by hanging cloth from the ceiling of the classroom. Pieces of doweling are glued or sewn to each end of the material. String or wire is attached to one end of the cloth and then to hooks inserted in the ceiling, or it is tied to the ceiling lights. The cloth divider also functions as a display area.

Box Office

Cutting out the top and bottom and one side of a large cardboard box forms an effective portable *office* where students can work alone. They can be assigned by the teacher or selected by the students, depending on when and why they are to be used. Students can also build and decorate their own box offices.

Teacher's Desk

The teacher's desk can be used by students as an extra place to store and file materials. The top of the desk can also become a student office. Arranging the desk as part of a learning or working area makes that desk a more usable piece of classroom furniture.

Closet Door

When a closet door is permanently left open, the door can become a bulletin board and the closet space can become an additional work or storage area. The closet door makes an ideal screen for reviewing film-strips. A learning center can be housed inside. Placing tables and chairs adjacent to the closet further enhances its usability.

Egg Carton

A soundproof room divider can be built by joining egg cartons with brads, tape, and staples. It can be suspended from the ceiling or supported by blocks of wood at its base.

Chipboard Divider

A divider can be made of durable cardboard and used as a bulletin board. Placing it between two tables makes two areas which can be used as learning centers.

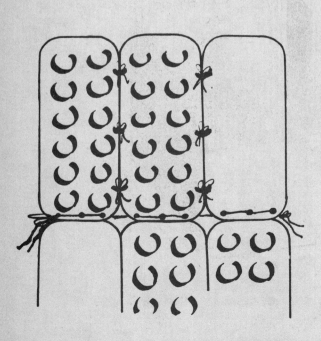

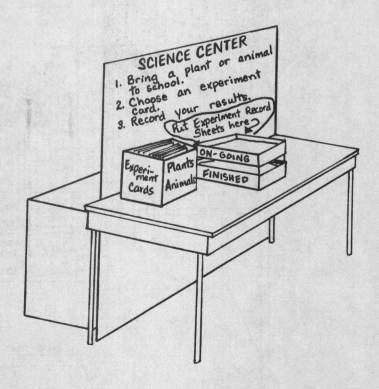

Room Divider

The nurse's screen or a flannel board are readymade dividers which can be used to section off working areas in the classroom. Making areas or corners out of open spaces provides for individual and group activities. The dividers themselves can function as display areas for student and teacher work.

Corrugated Booth

Corrugated paper can be used to design areas for students to work independently, to find quiet, or to isolate themselves from the group. The paper is taped along a table top to form individual study booths. Other types of heavy paper can be used.

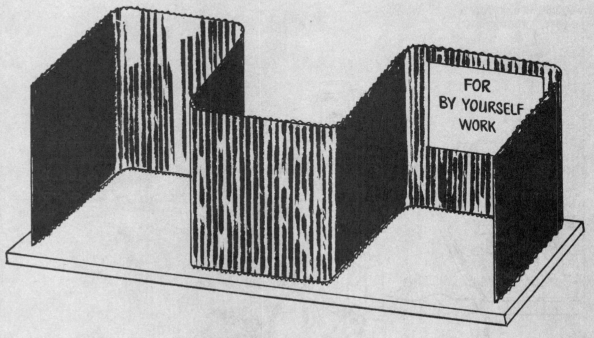

SIGNS AND LABELS

Posting signs and labeling areas focuses the students' attention on what and where things are in the room. Because signs and labels function like maps to direct students on their learning course, the teacher is free to spend more time on instruction. Their use also reinforces the skill of following and interpreting directions from written messages. Labeling and designating various areas of the classroom further the goal of developing self-directed learners.

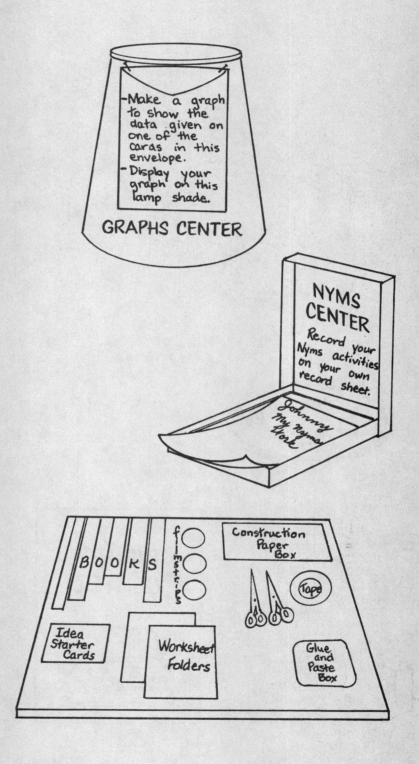

Lampshade

Worksheets, directions, lists of activities, and projects are a few examples of the types of items which can be displayed on a new or discarded lampshade. The teacher or student pins or tapes things he wishes to exhibit on the lampshade.

Bulletin Board Box

A storage area and bulletin board can be made by standing the lid of a dress or shirt box against the bottom of that box. Messages written or pinned on the bulletin board relate to the materials that are placed in the box.

Labeling A Center

The area on which a learning center will be displayed is covered with paper. A diagram is drawn on the paper to indicate where each of the materials for the center will be placed. Students can thus easily assume responsibility for the care of materials and the orderliness of the center.

Footprint Sign

Footprints cut and taped to the floor capture interest and direct students to an area in the classroom. Let students use their own feet as patterns.

Sign Post

Made of paper, doweling, and clay, sign posts call attention to working spaces or materials.

Poster

Posters made from heavy paper and posted or hung at the activities area help students to identify and locate the alternatives which are available to them. Artistically done posters magnetize students toward them and provide additional decor for the classroom.

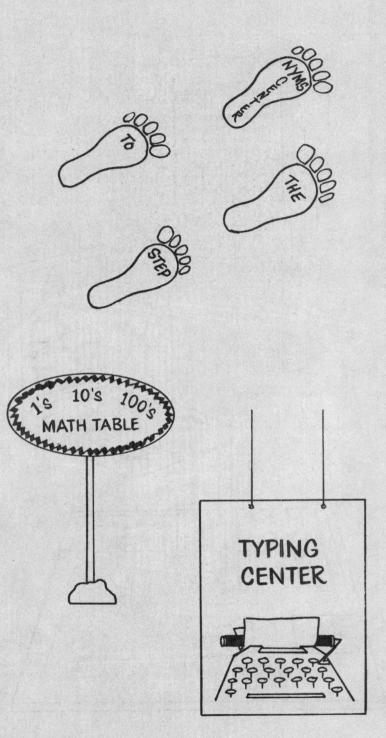

WAYS TO STORE MATERIALS

In order to allow students to become independent workers while maintaining an orderly classroom, the teacher needs to provide various ways to store materials. When materials are stored openly, children are able to direct their own activity without relying on the teacher. Careful labeling and placing of storage holders develops the students' awareness of where things can be found and how things should be kept. The labeling of materials reinforces student responsibility. Teachers should provide ways to store:

    childrens' belongings
    books
    supplies
    projects
    games
    files
    charts
    worksheets

Bottle Box

A divided carton makes a handy storage cupboard with each section identified by labels. Supplies, student projects, or materials can be placed in the bottle box.

Saw Horse

When a saw horse is turned upside down, its legs form bookends which can hold large pieces of chipboard, cardboard, and paper. This makes an ideal place to file cumbersome pictures and projects on a permanent or temporary basis. Pieces of cardboard labeled with children's names can be used as dividers for this filing cabinet.

File Box

Made out of cardboard boxes covered with wrapping or contact paper, the file boxes contain the materials for a specific curriculum area. Folders in the file box are labeled and placed in a meaningful sequence. A corrected example of each worksheet should be placed within the folder so that students can assume the responsibility for self-checking.

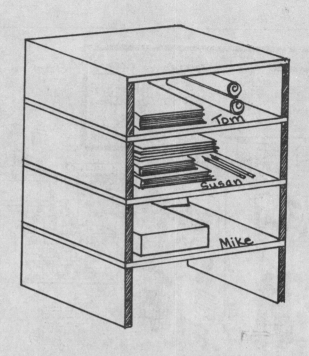

Cubbies

Produce boxes can be used as children's lockers, as bookcases, or as storage bins. Knock out one side then sand and paint them. They can be stacked and held secure with heavy-duty staples, nails driven in at an angle, or a strip of wood attached along the side.

Shoe Holder

Dimestore shoe holders can become storage centers for supplies or learning activity cards. Labeling the pockets helps the class locate and return materials.

DISPLAYING CHILDREN'S WORK

Displaying Work for Children

Making materials accessible to students is an essential part of helping them become self-directed. It also reinforces the development of the students' decision-making skills. Careful and artistic placement of materials serves to motivate students to use the materials. The teacher's arrangements of materials can also provide a standard for students to emulate when they display their own work.

Displaying Work of Children

The classroom environment should reflect the students who live and work in it. Displaying children's work helps to give recognition to each child as an individual. Each individual's contribution acts as a stimulus to others. A specific length of time for items to be exhibited insures that all can have an opportunity to display their work and that the classroom environment does not become static.

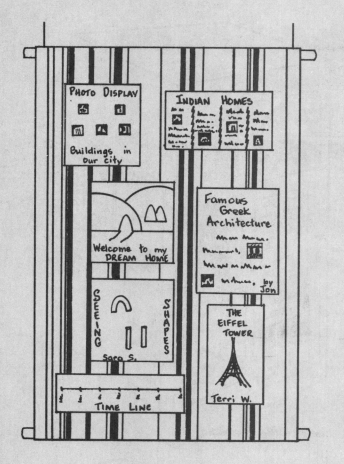

Wall Hanging

A piece of fabric stretched between two pieces of doweling serves as an additional bulletin board on which items may be displayed.

Clothesline

Tape or tack up colored yarn to make a clothesline for exhibiting work done by children or to bring attention to activities children can do. Paper or plastic bags can be used to hold art supplies, worksheets, or task cards for children to use.

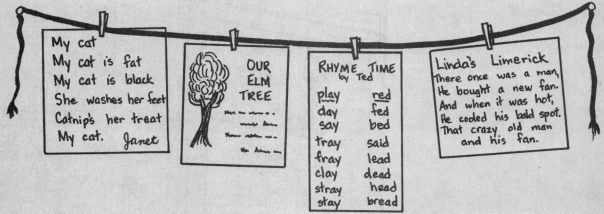

Refrigerator Box

A large box provides a free-standing display area. It can be moved to different locations within the room to become part of any learning or work center.

Cardboard Backdrop

Sheets of cardboard or plywood can be hinged together with masking tape to form a backdrop for exhibiting materials. This backdrop can also be used as a screen to section off areas on a table or on the floor.

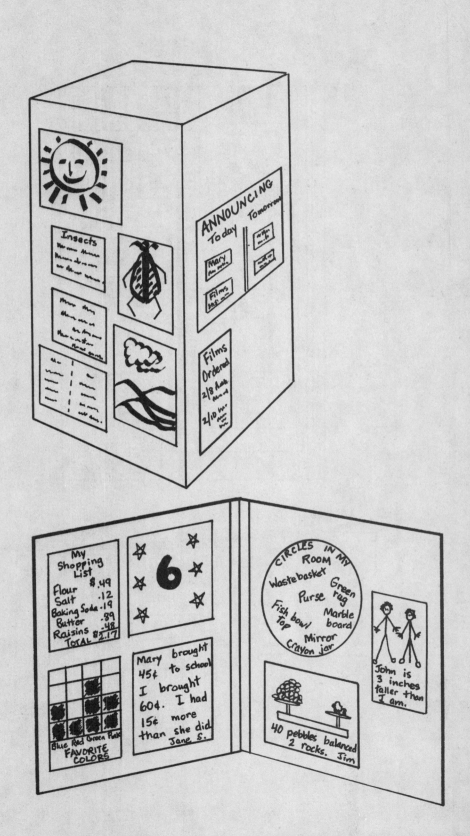

CONSTRUCTION	Building Materials
Human Resources	**Materials Available**
Bring & talk about building materials — Mr. Jones available Mon. afternoons	wood scraps, old nails, screws talk to Mr. Lee, ext. 45
Teaching sawing, nailing, drilling, etc. Mr. Lee call to arrange time	old linoleum samples, formica samples, broken bricks talk to Mr. Jones
Tour through Company — Mr. Zee call for appointment	
XYZ BUILDING SUPPLIES	262 huh Blvd — phone 326-2387

GETTING THINGS NEEDED FOR THE CLASSROOM

The concept of the *everywhere class-room* is that teachers and students can find tools for learning everywhere—in the community, neighborhood, and home. Locating objects for the classroom develops the student's awareness of his environment and helps him see the potential for the different uses of things. It is also a way for parents and the community to get involved in the school and recognize the changes taking place in education.

GARDENS — vegetables	
Human Resources	**Materials Available**
Demonstration of planting, caring for plants, harvesting Mrs. G. available on Tu, Thurs, 10-11 a.m.	Samples of seeds, plant leaves, stems, flowers
Visit to Mrs. G's garden— limit: 6 students per time call to set up time	Types of gardening tools — Some available for short term loan
Call for information anytime	Samples of fertilizers and soils for experiments.
Mrs. Gary — 624 Blue St. —	phone: 624-3888

Resource File

A resource file can be established to extend learnings beyond the limits of the classroom, the teacher's area of knowledge, and the reading material available at given levels. The need and use of such a file arises from student interest, independent study topics, and learning center themes and activities. The responsibility for soliciting resources should be both the teacher's and the student's. As resources are identified, the pertinent information is recorded on cards. This file enables students to have firsthand experiences by visiting places and to have direct contact with people who offer expertise.

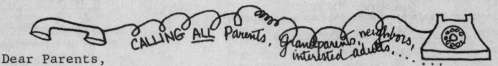

Dear Parents,

    Can you HELP us??? You may be surprised at the ways you can help and how much fun you'll have doing it. We already have 3 parents who are donating their time and resources. Don't worry about how much time you can give or how regularly you can come. We'll work something out.

    Following is a list of some of the ways you can help us. Maybe you have other ideas as well. Please check the areas where you can help and return this form to school with your child tomorrow.

    Thank you for your cooperation and interest.

Mrs. Jones

These materials will be used by the children and will not be returned, so don't give us your best!

_____ tin cans and plastic containers with lids
_____ cooking utensils (mixing bowls, measuring cups and spoons, etc.)
_____ lumber odds and ends, nails, screws
_____ tools (hammer, saw, pliers, screwdrivers)
_____ anything styrofoam (egg cartons, packing materials, etc.)
_____ needles and thread, spools, buttons
_____ T.V. dinner trays   _____ meat trays
_____ yarn and yardage scraps   _____ embroidery hoops
_____ rugs   _____ used furniture
_____ broken appliances

I can donate my time in the following ways:

____ help with clerical work (type stories at home, copy dittoes, etc.)
____ help in the classroom with small groups (no special skills needed)
____ help at the cooking center
____ help at the stitch and sew center
____ help children learn to shoot baskets, bat balls, jump rope, etc.)
____ help supervise on field trips and neighborhood walks
____ share a hobby, skill, interest or profession with the children
____ listen to an individual child read
____ take cans and bottles to the reclamation center

_____
Parent's signature

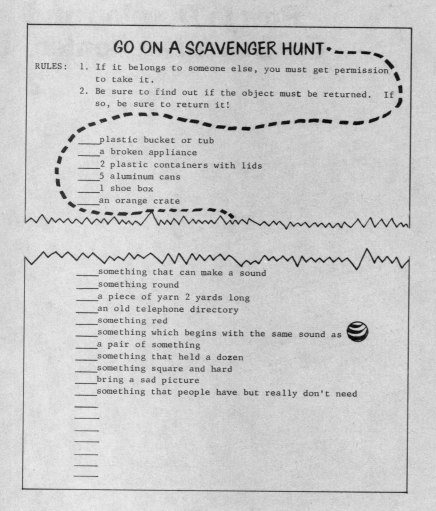

GO ON A SCAVENGER HUNT

RULES:
1. If it belongs to someone else, you must get permission to take it.
2. Be sure to find out if the object must be returned. If so, be sure to return it!

____plastic bucket or tub
____a broken appliance
____2 plastic containers with lids
____5 aluminum cans
____1 shoe box
____an orange crate

____something that can make a sound
____something round
____a piece of yarn 2 yards long
____an old telephone directory
____something red
____something which begins with the same sound as
____a pair of something
____something that held a dozen
____something square and hard
____bring a sad picture
____something that people have but really don't need

____
____
____
____
____
____
____

Scavenger Hunts

These scavenger hunts can be used as means of obtaining materials needed in the classroom or as an exciting way of reinforcing reading vocabulary and stimulating children's reasoning and thinking. Such lists might also be adapted to motivate and promote learning of a particular skill. For example, an Alphabet Center could be equipped with objects from home which match the sounds being studied. A list could be composed to teach and reinforce measurement. Scavenger hunts provide ways for children to actively participate in their learning.

How to Develop and Use Learning Centers

2

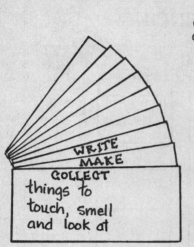

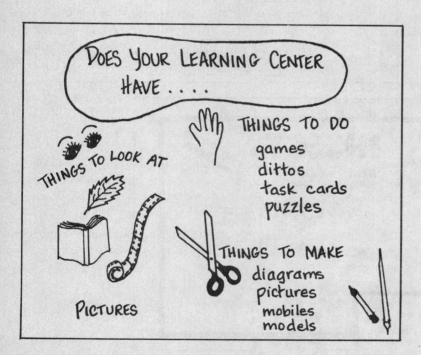

THE CHILD-CREATED LEARNING CENTER

The major purpose of the child-created learning center is to provide additional opportunities for individuals to explore and create. The center also allows students to help structure the classroom environment, increases student participation in learning, and stimulates opportunities for student recognition. The child-created learning center provides student-to-student communication and exchange. Students can be responsible for creating a new center or adding to an existing one. Individual students may develop centers as an outgrowth of independent study. Centers may also be developed by small groups as an assigned task or because of a common interest.

Coupon Book

Each coupon represents an ingredient in the learning center. A student selects a page in the coupon book, tears it out, and follows the directions on that page to add to his learning center.

Learning Center Model

Setting up a model for a learning center helps students visualize what components are necessary for their own learning centers. This model can serve as a reference for students throughout the year.

Announcing Pocket Chart

This chart announces happenings at the various child-created centers. It introduces students to new things at the centers and acts as a reminder for students to use in scheduling their own time.

ADD Chart

This chart gives recognition to students who will be contributing to the center. It reminds the students and the teacher of who has made a commitment to do an activity.

Open Bulletin Board

The students illustrate or write what they have learned at the center. As the board is filled, it becomes a mosaic of learnings.

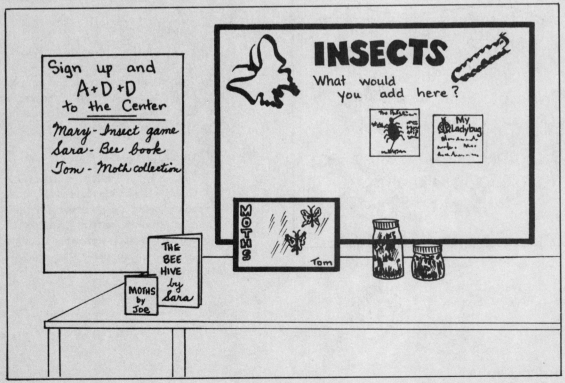

HOW TO TEACH A LESSON AT YOUR CENTER

Answer these questions before you teach.

1. What do I want to teach?

2. How will I spark interest for my lesson?

3. What materials will I need to use?

4. What will my teaching steps be?

5. What will students do or make after the lesson?

6. How will I evaluate my lesson?

CENTER:

What I liked to do best:

What I liked to do least:

What I would have added to the Center:

Child Taught Lessons

To encourage sharing and to spark interest in a center, students can teach their classmates. Provide students with a guide to assist them in organizing and presenting their lessons. It will help to insure a high quality lesson and success for the "teacher."

Center Evaluation

Students use this instrument to evaluate the learning center and give feedback to those who created the center. It also emphasizes the concept that learning centers belong to the class and, thus, can be modified according to class suggestions and needs.

AN INTRODUCTION TO LEARNING CENTERS

A learning center varies in its purpose just as it varies in its make-up.

Centers can be classified according to the teacher's purpose for their use. Some centers direct students toward the learning of specific knowledge or skills. Some stress the development of thinking and learning processes. Other centers employ topics, techniques, and tools which capture the student's enthusiasm and entice him to participate in learning.

The make-up of a learning center changes according to the purpose and type of the center. Each center will have a different variety and quantity of activities: games, worksheets, and manipulative activities. The placement of a center changes according to its use. Some centers are displayed on tables while others can be stored in boxes and brought out periodically. Individual students or groups may work at centers at various times during the day.

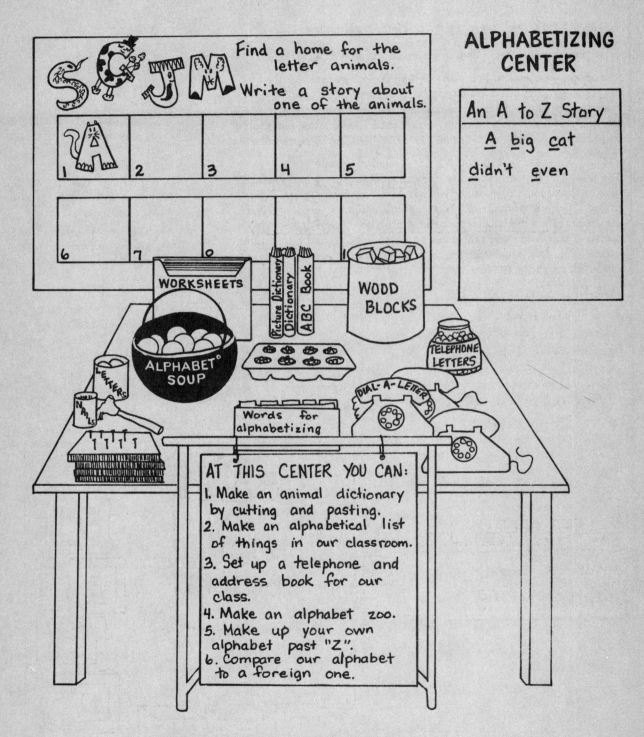

ALPHABETIZING CENTER

An A to Z Story

<u>A</u> <u>b</u>ig <u>c</u>at
<u>d</u>idn't <u>e</u>ven

Find a home for the letter animals.

Write a story about one of the animals.

1   2   3   4   5

6   7   8

WORKSHEETS

ALPHABET SOUP

Picture Dictionary
Dictionary
ABC Book

WOOD BLOCKS

TELEPHONE LETTERS

LETTERS

NAILS

Words for alphabetizing

DIAL-A-LETTER

AT THIS CENTER YOU CAN:
1. Make an animal dictionary by cutting and pasting.
2. Make an alphabetical list of things in our classroom.
3. Set up a telephone and address book for our class.
4. Make an alphabet zoo.
5. Make up your own alphabet past "Z".
6. Compare our alphabet to a foreign one.

Learning Possibilities

Recognizing the names of letters
Learning the sequence of the alphabet
Learning to alphabetize
Developing ability to use various kinds of dictionaries

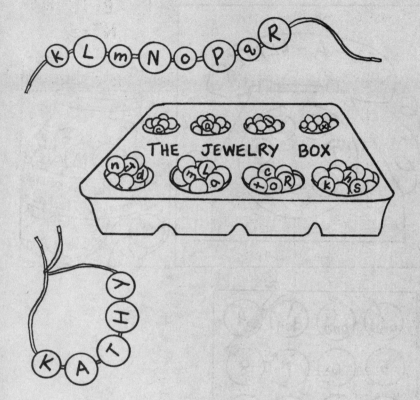

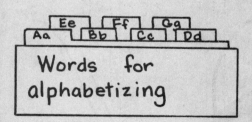

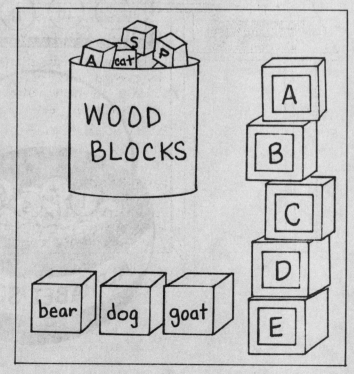

GAMES AND ACTIVITIES

1. Write letters on wooden beads of various sizes and colors. A muffin tin or divided box may be used as the "jewelry box." Children use yarn or string to string beads in alphabetical order or to spell words.

2. Place dividers for each letter of the alphabet in a box. Children add word cards to the box behind the appropriate divider.

Another independent activity would be for children to remove all the cards from the box, shuffle, and re-alphabetize them.

3. Tape words and letters on small plain blocks. Children arrange letter or word blocks in alphabetical sequence.

4. Draw telephones on heavy cardboard. Write letters on paper circles and put them in a container. Children draw letters from the container and arrange them in alphabetical order on the telephone dial.

Putting several cardboard telephones at the center would make it possible for children to play a game. The first child to alphabetize his letters correctly is the winner.

5. Draw or paint several numbered circles on a board. Write words on paper circles and place them in a container. Children take several words, arrange them in alphabetical order, and nail them to the appropriate spaces on the board.

6. Write letters on paper circles or squares and place them in a cooking pot. Children ladle out letters and arrange them in alphabetical order.

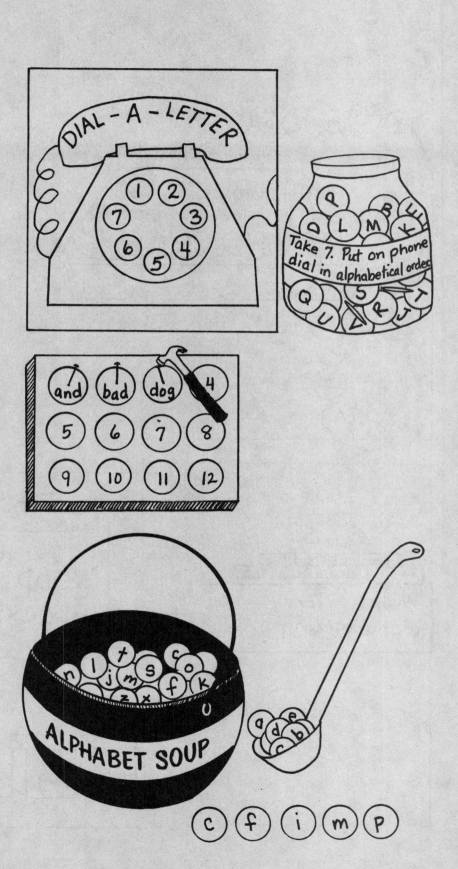

WORKSHEETS

BE A GOOD GARDENER

Grow the flowers in ABC order in the flower pot.

E

R

C

A

V

L

N

F

SEND A TELEGRAM

Cut words from magazines and newspapers. Paste them in alphabetical order to make up a telegram to send to a friend.

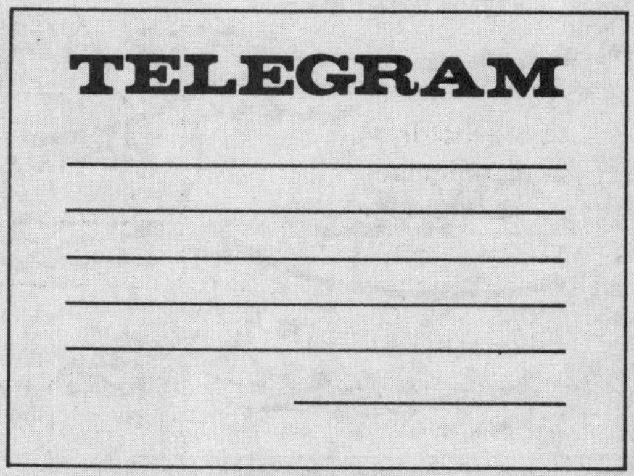

TELEGRAM

CAN YOU FILL THE ALPHABET WORM?

Cut and paste in alphabetical order according to the first 2 letters.

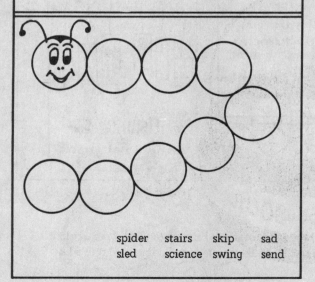

| spider | stairs | skip | sad |
| sled | science | swing | send |

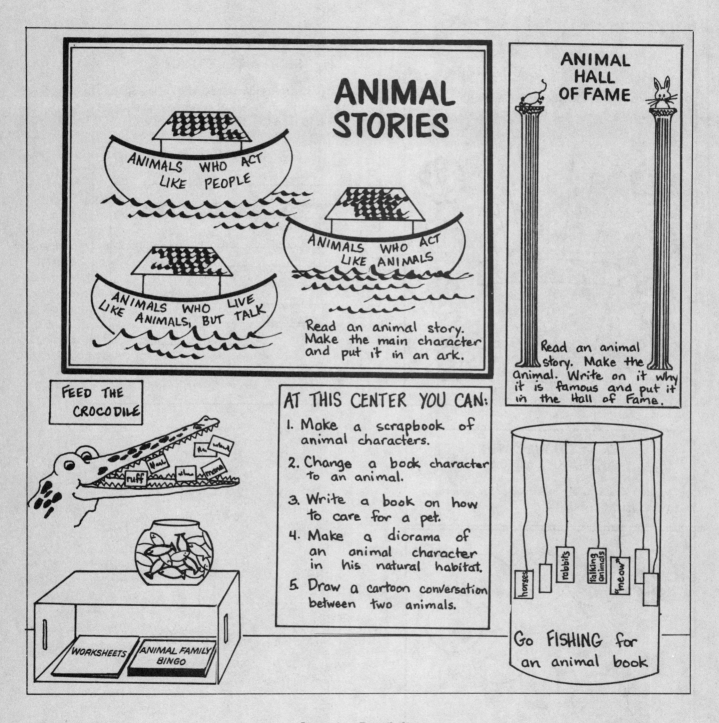

Learning Possibilities

Learning the three types of animal stories (animals who act like people, animals who act like animals, and animals who live like animals, but talk)

Stimulating reading and creative writing

Developing vocabulary

Developing the skill of transforming one thing to another

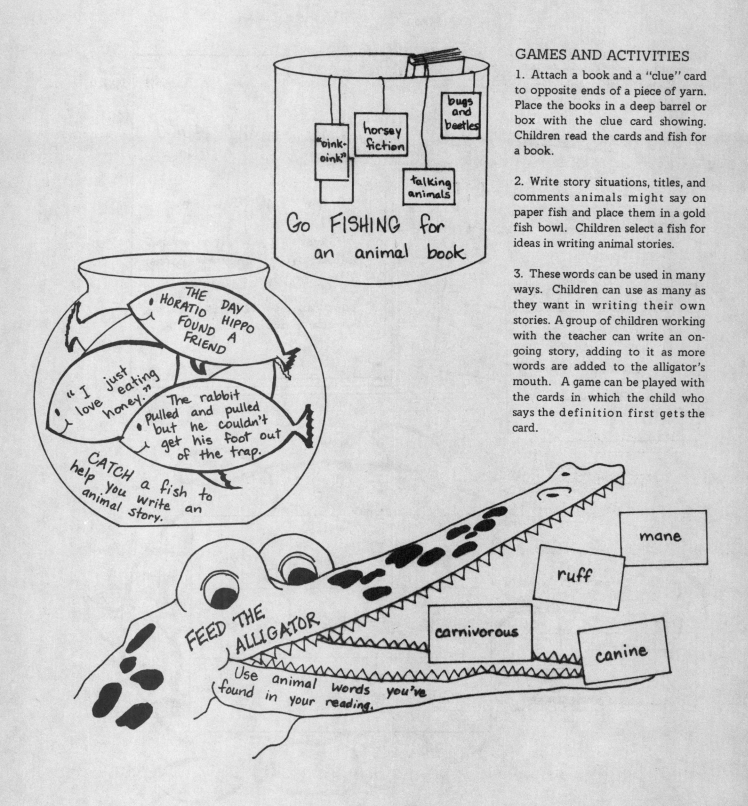

GAMES AND ACTIVITIES

1. Attach a book and a "clue" card to opposite ends of a piece of yarn. Place the books in a deep barrel or box with the clue card showing. Children read the cards and fish for a book.

2. Write story situations, titles, and comments animals might say on paper fish and place them in a gold fish bowl. Children select a fish for ideas in writing animal stories.

3. These words can be used in many ways. Children can use as many as they want in writing their own stories. A group of children working with the teacher can write an on-going story, adding to it as more words are added to the alligator's mouth. A game can be played with the cards in which the child who says the definition first gets the card.

4. Make turtle-shaped playing cards with the names of animals in each square. On the set of caller's cards write the terms these animal families are called.

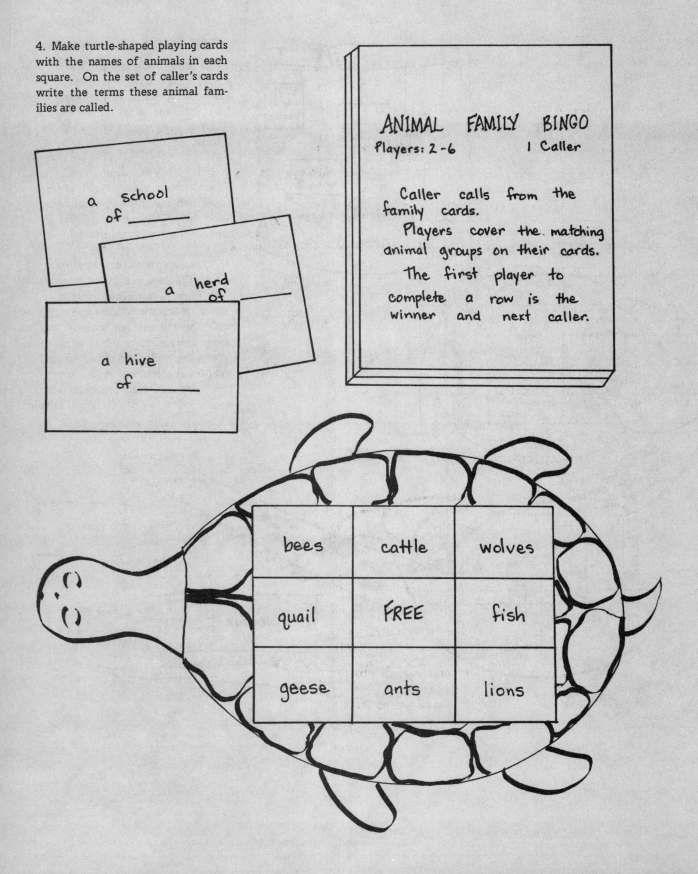

a school of _____

a herd of _____

a hive of _____

ANIMAL FAMILY BINGO
Players: 2-6   1 Caller

Caller calls from the family cards.

Players cover the matching animal groups on their cards.

The first player to complete a row is the winner and next caller.

bees	cattle	wolves
quail	FREE	fish
geese	ants	lions

WORKSHEETS

ANIMAL KINGDOM SURVEY

Show which animals appear most often in animal stories. Read animal stories and survey your friends.

STORIES	ANIMALS					
	dogs	bears	toads			
Wind in the Willows			1			
Lassie	1					

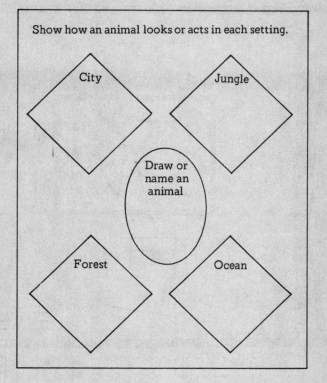

Show how an animal looks or acts in each setting.

City

Jungle

Draw or name an animal

Forest

Ocean

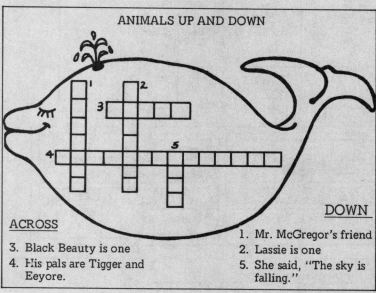

ANIMALS UP AND DOWN

ACROSS

3. Black Beauty is one
4. His pals are Tigger and Eeyore.

DOWN

1. Mr. McGregor's friend
2. Lassie is one
5. She said, "The sky is falling."

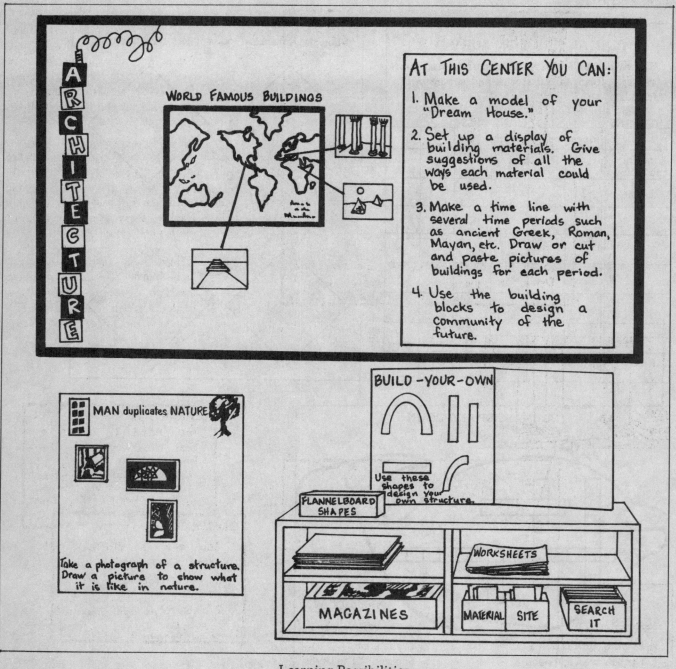

Learning Possibilities

Becoming acquainted with some basic architectural forms: arches, columns, flying buttresses, beams, etc.

Learning about famous structures and their locations in the world.

Reinforcing the concepts that man adapts to his natural environment as well as changes his environment to fit his needs.

Learning about how and why things change by considering the past, present, and future.

Take a photograph of a structure. Draw a picture to show what it is like in nature.

GAMES AND ACTIVITIES

1. Children take photographs of buildings which in some way duplicate or utilize nature in their construction. Then they make drawings to show the natural object, e.g., a bowl-shaped building duplicates a seashell.

2. Children research well-known buildings of the world and use yarn to show their locations on a world map hung at the center. A time should be made available for children to share what they learned about the buildings.

3. Make task cards about housing or buildings in various geographical locations. Questions should pertain to the materials found in each area and how they affect what is built there.

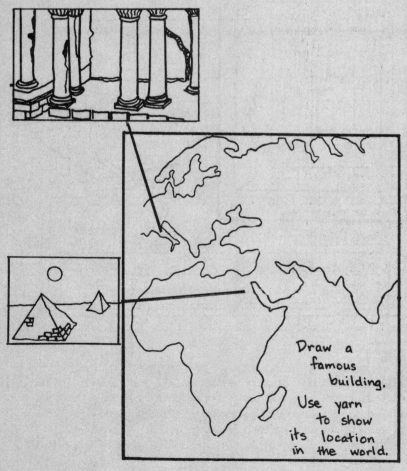

Draw a famous building.

Use yarn to show its location in the world.

SEARCH IT - - - - - - 2

You need to make a cost breakdown for the Empire State Building.

1. What materials were used?

2. What would they cost today?

SEARCH IT - - - - - - 1

You are a Plains Indian. You need a home.

1. What materials are available to you?

2. What style will you use? Why?

Source of Information:

4. Use flannel to make the basic architectural shapes such as arches, flying buttresses, columns, beams, and rafters. Children use these on a flannel board to build a structure.

5. Children cut out pictures of buildings from magazines. Using markers, they outline the basic shapes used in the buildings.

6. Make two sets of cards, one with unusual sites and one with raw materials. Children choose a site and materials and build a miniature shelter on the simulated location.

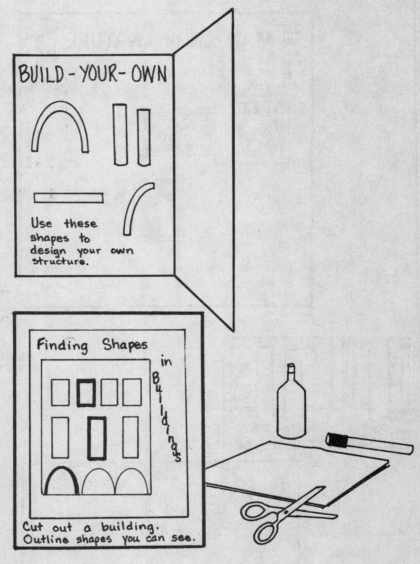

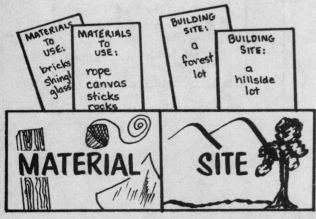

WORKSHEETS

DESIGNS, INC.

Memo:

Below is our design for the architectural conference's contest on the "Home of the Future."

FROM CAVE TO SKYSCRAPER

Show what changes took place.

Walk around your neighborhood.
Find buildings which use examples of these:

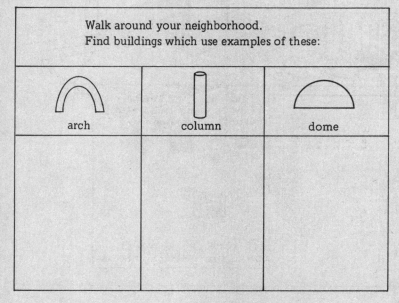

arch	column	dome

Learning Possibilities

Developing and appreciation of art
Recognizing various elements of art—line, texture, color, and form
Learning about different artists and styles of art
Experimenting with various media, techniques, and styles of art

GAMES AND ACTIVITIES

1. Make a portfolio with two pieces of cardboard taped at the bottom. Cover with contact paper, and add string or ribbon to close the top. Children copy a famous painting or find a print of it and file it in the portfolio according to the topic headings.

2. Place copies of a palette at the art center. In the circles children write the characteristics of an artist or of his paintings.

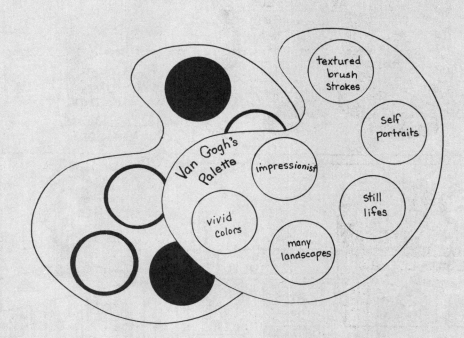

3. Collect materials such as a vase, artificial flowers, plastic fruit, branches, bottles, pieces of fabric, and bowls for the still life box.

4. Children mix colors to match those in a print they have chosen. They paint each color on a circle of paper and hang all the circles together with the print.

5. Collect art postcards for children to classify and tape in the rooms of the art museum. Children can make a sculpture garden and add their own creations to it.

STILL LIFE BOX
1. Choose several objects.
2. Arrange them in an interesting way.
3. Use paint, chalk, crayons, or charcoal to draw your arrangement.

Colors from Picasso's Three Masked Musicians

SCULPTURE GARDEN

CLASSIC

IMPRESSIONIST

MODERN

WORKSHEETS

Choose a painting in one of these styles. Draw it in its correct frame. Change it to show how it would look in one or both of the other styles.

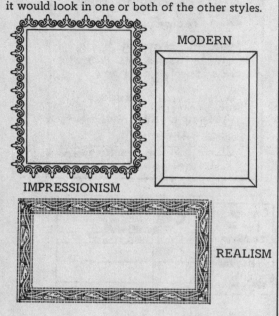

MODERN

IMPRESSIONISM

REALISM

1. Choose a painting.
2. List all the words which describe the painting in the frame.
3. See if someone else can guess which painting you have "framed."

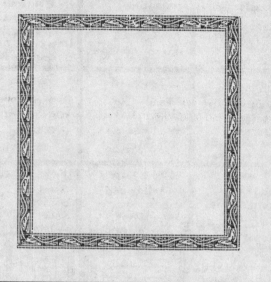

Copy or create a picture which uses each type of line as its main part.

COOKING CENTER

Tic-Tac-Dough 3 in a row means you cook.

Keep track of the foods you eat for 1 week. Chart or graph them into the 4 food groups.	Use magazine pictures to make a food collage.	Make a Table of Equivalent Measures. Do your own experimenting or use a cookbook.
Make a chart of all the foods made from 1 basic food... such as products made from potatoes	Copy a recipe on a card for the Recipe File.	Design a new packaging for a food product.
Tell why a food is packaged the way it is.	Make up a balanced menu for breakfast, lunch, and dinner.	Make a calorie count of one of your meals.

Getting Ready to Cook
1. Read recipe carefully.
2. Make a "shopping list". Collect ingredients from the class supply or home.
3. Wash your hands.
4. Assemble all ingredients and equipment.
5. Clear off a work area and get started!

Choose 1 or 2 cooking partners before you sign up.

Cooking Sign-up

Mon.	Tues.	Wed.	Thurs.	Fri.

What Every Gourmet Cook Needs to Know

Recipe File

Cookbook

Potato Chips

SUGAR SALT BROWN SUGAR SOAP

Cooking Research Cards

Learning Possibilities

Learning about foods and nutrition

Learning planning and organizing through cooking

Developing ability to follow directions

Learning to use volume measurements

Working cooperatively with others

The Basic 4 food families are shown on the right.

Find food "friends" from the envelope below to fill each family.

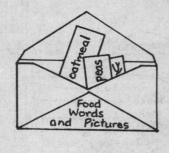

FOOD FAMILY "FRIENDS"

Vegetables and Fruits	Milk and Milk Products
Breads and Cereals	Meat Poultry Fish

GAMES AND ACTIVITIES

1. Paste an envelope on the inside of a manila folder. Fill it with food words and pictures. On the adjacent side write the names of the food groups. An answer sheet can be placed inside the envelope.

2. Write the name of a food on one card and its source on another. Make at least thirteen food pairs.

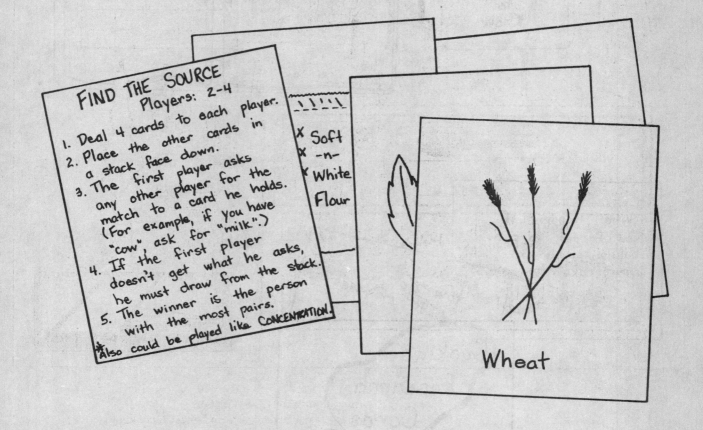

FIND THE SOURCE
Players: 2-4

1. Deal 4 cards to each player.
2. Place the other cards in a stack face down.
3. The first player asks any other player for the match to a card he holds. (For example, if you have "cow", ask for "milk".)
4. If the first player doesn't get what he asks, he must draw from the stack.
5. The winner is the person with the most pairs.
*Also could be played like CONCENTRATION.

Soft
-n-
White
Flour

Wheat

3. This book contains two sections, *The ABC's of Cooking* and *Kitchen Hints*. Children add cooking terms and their definitions to the first section and helpful hints they have learned in cooking to the second section.

4. Children answer the questions on the research cards. They may also add a question to the research file.

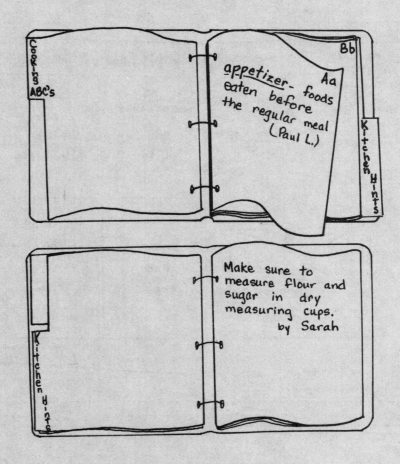

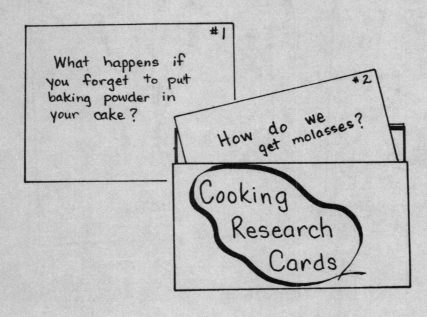

WORKSHEETS

INTERNATIONAL FOOD MENU

Food	Country	Price
Sukiyaki	Japan	50 yen
Tacos		
Paella		
Crepes Suzette		
Frankfurters		
Spaghetti		

What can you add to this menu?

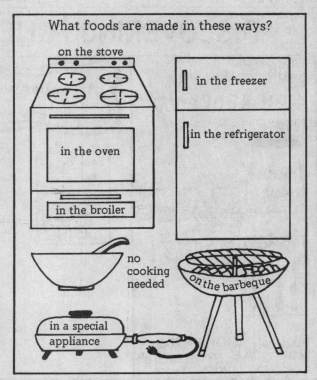

What foods are made in these ways?

on the stove

in the freezer

in the oven

in the refrigerator

in the broiler

no cooking needed

on the barbeque

in a special appliance

Can you find these equivalents in a book or figure them out yourself?

How many tablespoons in ½ cup? _____ T. = ½ cup

How many ounces in a cup? _____ oz. = 1 c.

How many cups in a quart? _____ c. = 1 qt.

How many cubes of butter in a pound? _____ cubes = 1 lb.

Find other equivalents and add them to the list.

DISCOVERING A NEIGHBORHOOD

ALL IN A NEIGHBORHOOD

TRASH WALK

Colors of Houses

MY BIRD WALK

Take a NEIGHBORHOOD WALK. Add something from your walk to this board.

Neighborhood Interviews

Sam S., gardener

WANTED for the NEIGHBORHOOD

WANTED A bicycle rack for the vacant lot.

MAKE A WANTED NOTICE FOR SOMETHING NEEDED IN YOUR NEIGHBORHOOD

WANTED A new style telephone pole

AT THIS CENTER YOU CAN:

1. Make up a "walk" form for someone to take ... such as A Noise Walk, or A Tree Walk.

2. Make a graph of something in the neighborhood.

3. Be a neighborhood surveyor. Collect such measurements as: heights of trees, lengths of driveways.

4. Write a neighborhood history, by interviewing, reading old newspapers, ...

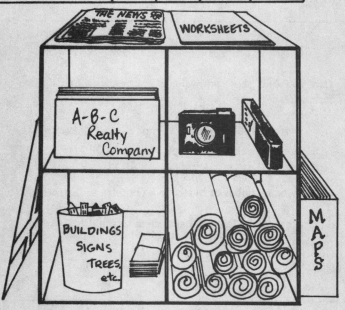

THE NEWS

WORKSHEETS

A-B-C Realty Company

BUILDINGS SIGNS TREES, etc.

MAPS

Learning Possibilities

Developing an awareness and involvement in one's own neighborhood

Developing the ability to be a careful observer

Learning about how people affect the nature of a neighborhood

Exploring alternatives for effecting change in a neighborhood

Applying measurement and map skills

GAMES AND ACTIVITIES

1. Place a box with large index cards in it at the center. After taking a walk in the neighborhood, children write out data cards. They should include a drawing of the front of the house or a floor plan. Children may gather the information from looking at the house or from talking to people who live in it.

2. After a group walk, a student may make his own mural of part of the neighborhood. Using butcher paper, he may include three or four houses, an entire block, a shopping center, or whatever else he wants. He may concentrate on some aspect studied by the class or on a specialized interest, such as plants, measurements, or building styles.

3. The teacher designs a board showing blocks, streets, and directions. She provides toy buildings, signs, trees, etc. for use on the board.

The cards and board may be used several ways: as a small group lesson with the teacher; as an individual, independent activity; or as a small group competitive game. To use as a competitive game, cards may carry points, depending on difficulty. Each player decides to try a more difficult or an easier card. He follows the directions and keeps the card. When the game is finished, a completed map (made by the teacher to fit the cards) is used to decide which players earn points.

4. A cassette recorder may be used in a variety of ways on walks: to describe a house, building, or yard; to tape walking directions to a certain location which may be tested out by another child; to interview neighbors, storekeepers, or community helpers; to record neighborhood sounds in various locations; to tape children's comments as they view a specific object (newly poured cement, a mailbox, a beehive, etc.).

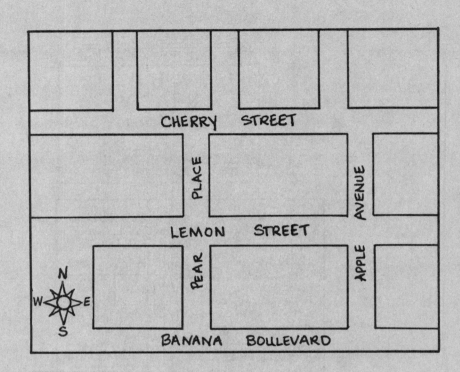

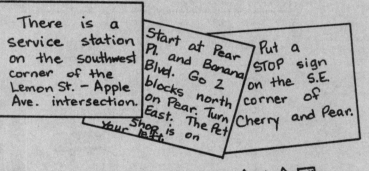

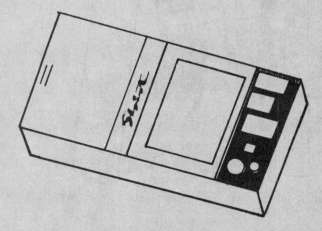

WORKSHEETS

Design a new house from those around you. Choose each feature from a different house in your neighborhood.

Design a Home

Features you may wish to include:

door	walkway	steps
porch	T.V. antenna	chimney
mail box	and ? ? ?	

Categorize

All of the items on one location (a home, a store, a yard, a church).

Wood   Growing things
_____   _____

Cement, brick, plaster   Glass
_____   _____

Metal   Plastic
_____   _____

_____   _____

ALIKE > and < DIFFERENT

Choose 6 houses on a block. Use words or drawings to compare a feature of the houses, such as T.V. antennas, doors, windows or shrubbery. Look for things that are alike and different.

FAIRY TALES

The Fairy Tale Castle

EVENTS HAPPENING IN 3'S

HAPPY ENDING

"ONCE UPON A TIME"

MAGIC

GOOD & BAD CHARACTERS

Each flag has on it an ingredient of a fairy tale.

Find these ingredients in a fairy tale you have read and put them in the right part of the castle.

FAIRY TALE PICTURE BOOK

Pick a story idea

AT THIS CENTER YOU CAN:

1. Write a want-ad for a fairy tale character.

2. Make a puppet of a fairy tale character.

3. Dress up a friend as one of your favorite fairy tale characters. See if others can guess who it is.

4. Make your own dot-to-dot ditto of a character for others to do.

5. Write a modern fairy tale that could take place today.

Learning Possibilities

Learning the elements of a fairy tale (events happening in threes, happy ending, magic, "once upon a time," good and bad characters)

Enjoying fairy tales

Learning about the elements of character and setting in stories, and developing them in original story writing

Stimulating imaginative writing and thinking

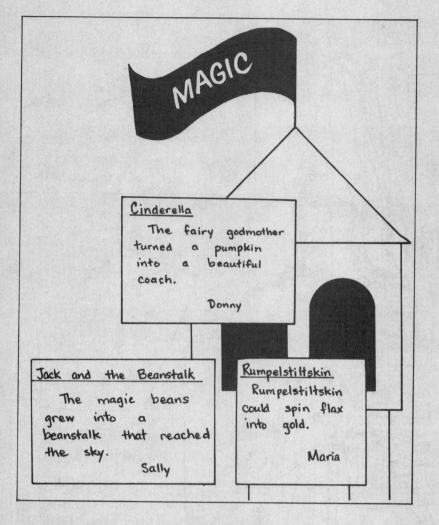

GAMES AND ACTIVITIES

1. Children may use any fairy tale they have read to illustrate the ingredients of a fairy tale.

2. Make a book out of large pieces of colored construction paper. Paste pictures of objects, people, or settings on alternate pages of the book. Children select one of the pictures and write or draw about how the picture could be used in a fairy tale.

3. Write the title of a fairy tale on one half of a large card and an event that occurs in it on the other half. Cut the halves apart using a different jigsaw pattern for each card.

4. Children may write alone or with others. A child who has difficulty in writing may ask another child to help him.

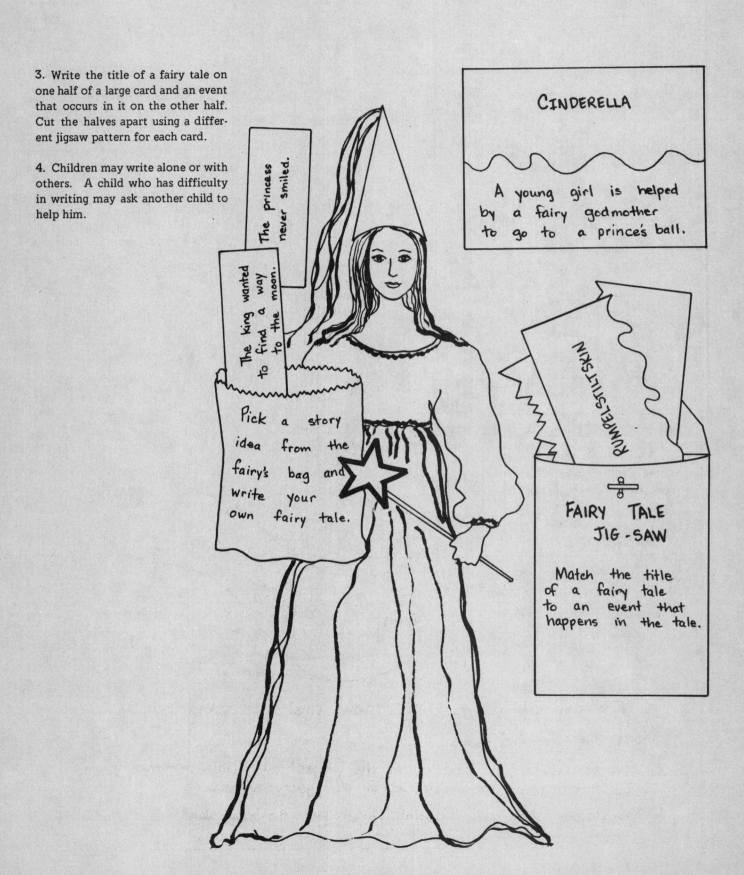

The princess never smiled.

The king wanted to find a way to the moon.

Pick a story idea from the fairy's bag and write your own fairy tale.

CINDERELLA

A young girl is helped by a fairy godmother to go to a prince's ball.

RUMPELSTILTSKIN

FAIRY TALE JIG-SAW

Match the title of a fairy tale to an event that happens in the tale.

5. Following the directions on the game, children use their imaginations and vocabularies to make up the longest fairy tale sentences they can. These do not have to come from fairy tales they have read.

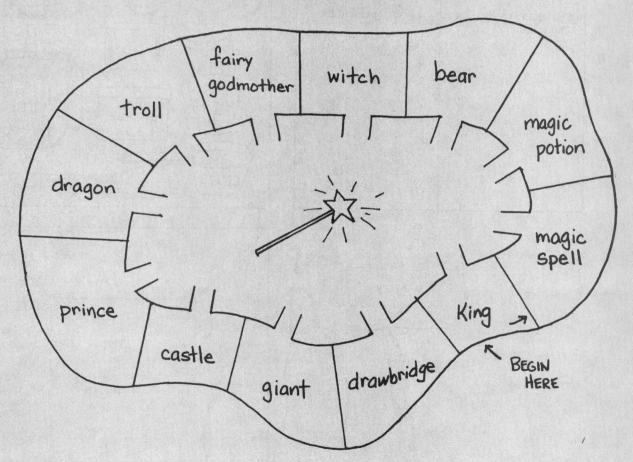

CAPTURE THE MAGIC WAND

Who can get to the Magic Wand first? It takes 40 points.

1. Roll the die and move.
2. Use the word you land on in the longest fairy tale sentence you can. You get 1 point for each word in your sentence.
3. The player who gets 40 points first gets the Magic Wand.

Show which parts of a fairy tale are believable and which parts are make believe.

Story Title: <u>Little Red Riding Hood</u>

Believable Parts	Make Believe Parts
a girl going to visit her grandmother	a wolf that can talk

Color in the ingredients you would add to a fairy tale.

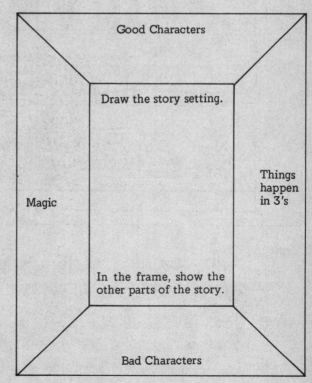

Good Characters

Draw the story setting.

Magic

Things happen in 3's

In the frame, show the other parts of the story.

Bad Characters

GRAPHS

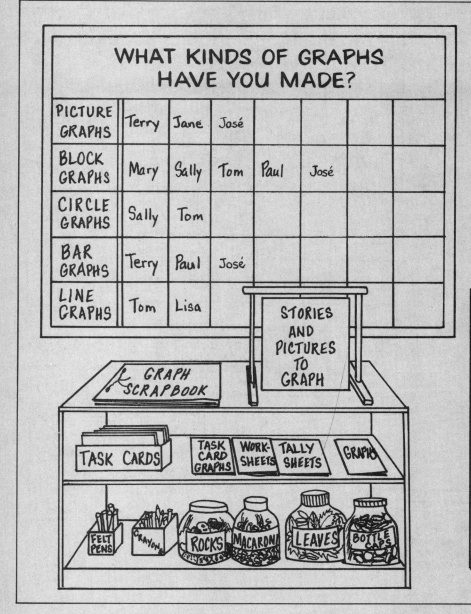

WHAT KINDS OF GRAPHS HAVE YOU MADE?

PICTURE GRAPHS	Terry	Jane	José			
BLOCK GRAPHS	Mary	Sally	Tom	Paul	José	
CIRCLE GRAPHS	Sally	Tom				
BAR GRAPHS	Terry	Paul	José			
LINE GRAPHS	Tom	Lisa				

GRAPH SCRAPBOOK

STORIES AND PICTURES TO GRAPH

TASK CARDS

TASK CARD GRAPHS · WORK-SHEETS · TALLY SHEETS · GRAPHS

FELT PENS · CRAYONS · ROCKS · MACARONI · LEAVES · BOTTLE CAPS

COUNTS TO TAKE IN THE ROOM

Color of hair
Color of eyes
Color of shoes
Streets children live on
Kinds of books on the shelves
Kinds of pets

AT THIS CENTER YOU CAN:

1. Find a graph in a magazine. Explain it to a friend. Add it to the graph scrapbook.

2. Make a graph showing something you have counted.

3. Make a list of ideas for someone else to graph.

4. Collect things to graph.

Learning Possibilities

Understanding that graphing is a method of comparing numbers
Familiarizing children with different types of graphs
Interpreting graphs
Making graphs
Counting

GAMES AND ACTIVITIES

1. Children listen to a story which is read by the teacher or another child, or has been put on tape. Children keep a tally sheet of all the times they hear a certain word or phrase. Later they are asked to graph their findings. Another step would be to make up story problems from the information tallied.

2. A set of task cards can be made up about number stories and problems. A folder with worksheets numbered to correspond with the task cards is kept next to the task card file box.

3. This chart rack has stories and pictures containing number situations which may be graphed by children. Small groups of children can work with the teacher to create the stories.

TALLY	SHEET	
cat	red	fast

Name: ③

Mrs. 7	▨	▨	▨	▨	▨	▨	▨
Mr. 4	▨	▨	▨	▨			
	1	2	3	4	5	6	7	8

GRAPH TASK CARD ③

Mrs. 7 and Mr. 4 were talking. Mrs. 7 said, "I am larger than you are." Mr. 4 said, "Prove it."

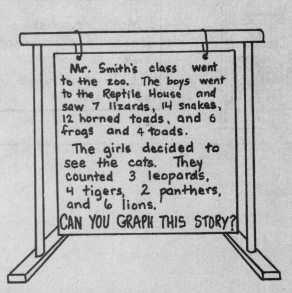

Mr. Smith's class went to the zoo. The boys went to the Reptile House and saw 7 lizards, 14 snakes, 12 horned toads, and 6 frogs and 4 toads.

The girls decided to see the cats. They counted 3 leopards, 4 tigers, 2 panthers, and 6 lions.

CAN YOU GRAPH THIS STORY?

WORKSHEETS

My Friends' Pets			
Dogs	Cats	Birds	Fish

Cut out these pictures and paste them on the graph.

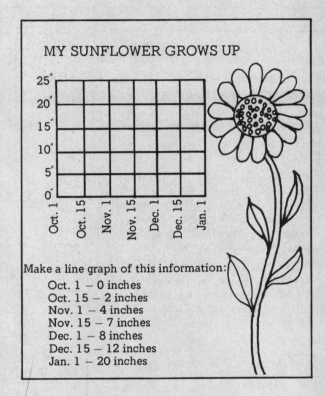

MY SUNFLOWER GROWS UP

Make a line graph of this information:

Oct. 1 — 0 inches
Oct. 15 — 2 inches
Nov. 1 — 4 inches
Nov. 15 — 7 inches
Dec. 1 — 8 inches
Dec. 15 — 12 inches
Jan. 1 — 20 inches

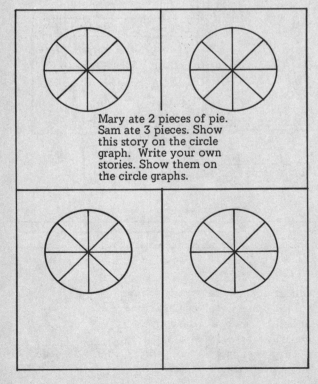

Mary ate 2 pieces of pie. Sam ate 3 pieces. Show this story on the circle graph. Write your own stories. Show them on the circle graphs.

handwriting

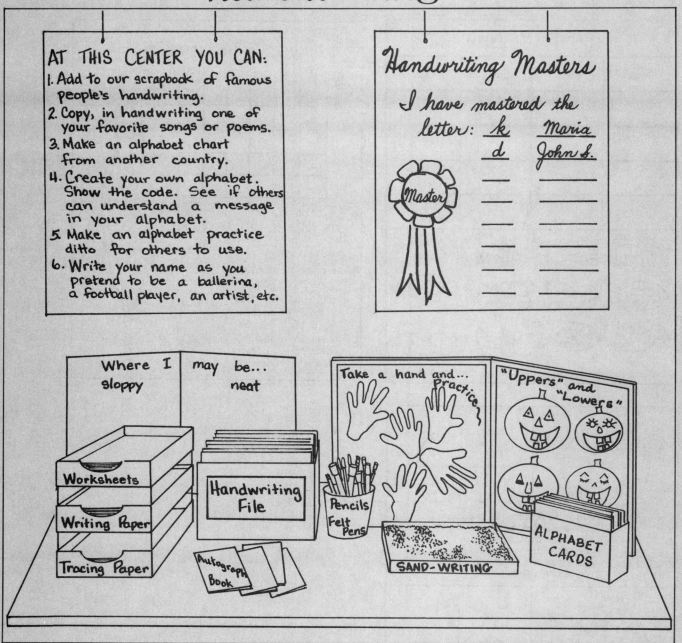

AT THIS CENTER YOU CAN:
1. Add to our scrapbook of famous people's handwriting.
2. Copy, in handwriting one of your favorite songs or poems.
3. Make an alphabet chart from another country.
4. Create your own alphabet. Show the code. See if others can understand a message in your alphabet.
5. Make an alphabet practice ditto for others to use.
6. Write your name as you pretend to be a ballerina, a football player, an artist, etc.

Handwriting Masters

I have mastered the letter: k   Maria
d   John S.

Master

Where I may be...
sloppy   neat

Worksheets

Writing Paper

Tracing Paper

Handwriting File

Autograph Book

Pencils Felt Pens

Take a hand and... Practice!

SAND-WRITING

"Uppers" and "Lowers"

ALPHABET CARDS

Learning Possibilities

Recognizing manuscript and cursive letter forms
Learning some of the principles of legible writing
Developing a kinesthetic sense of letter forms
Learning to write legibly and with ease
Learning that the degree of care taken in written work is dependent on who will read it or how it will be used

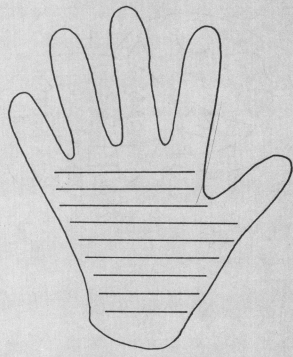

GAMES AND ACTIVITIES

1. The handwriting file contains worksheets that are grouped according to a skill or a specific letter. The dividers, showing the skill or letter at the top, enable children to select for themselves the worksheets they need to practice.

2. Staple paper together to make an autograph book. Children collect the autographs of classmates written in their best handwriting.

3. Ditto a hand with writing lines on it on construction paper or ditto paper. Children use the hands for practicing handwriting.

4. Fill the lid of a heavy box half full with sand. Students practice writing letters or words in the sand.

5. Make pumpkins with tagboard, and cover them with clear contact. Children place or write corresponding manuscript and cursive letters on the teeth.

6. Buy or make your own alphabet cards. Cover them with clear contact. Children may trace over the letters with their index fingers or with an erasable plastic crayon.

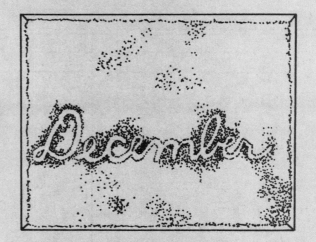

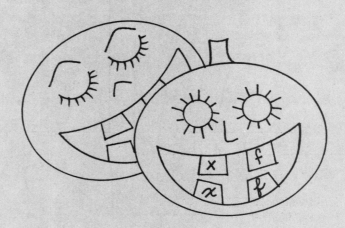

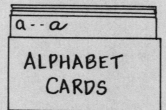

WORKSHEETS

Practice: your name
or
a word
or
a letter

Make it into a cartoon character.

TRACE–PRACTICE–PERFECT
1. Choose a letter to practice.
2. Have the teacher write it for you.
3. Trace the letter as many times as you need to.

Trace   Practice   Write your perfect letter

HANDWRITING SCORE SHEET

Rules	Write sentences or a paragraph here:	Score
2 points for all letters on line		
1 point for closing letters a, d, g		
3 points for even slant / / / /		
2 points for even height arm		
2 points for not looping these letters d, t, i	Total Score	

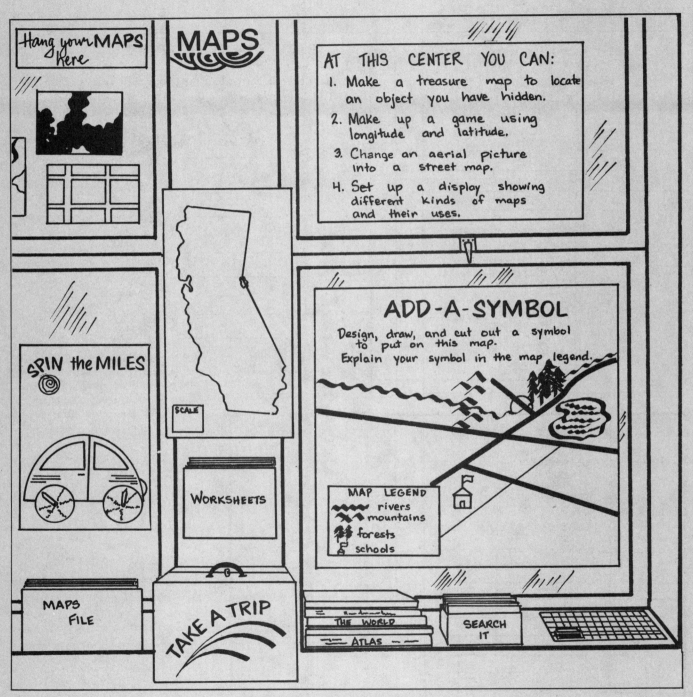

Hang your MAPS here

MAPS

AT THIS CENTER YOU CAN:

1. Make a treasure map to locate an object you have hidden.

2. Make up a game using longitude and latitude.

3. Change an aerial picture into a street map.

4. Set up a display showing different kinds of maps and their uses.

SCALE

SPIN the MILES

WORKSHEETS

ADD-A-SYMBOL

Design, draw, and cut out a symbol to put on this map.

Explain your symbol in the map legend.

MAP LEGEND
rivers
mountains
forests
schools

MAPS FILE

TAKE A TRIP

THE WORLD

ATLAS

SEARCH IT

Learning Possibilities

Extending knowledge of geography
Identifying and interpreting various kinds of maps
Using map legends, scales, and latitude and longitude
Making maps
Applying math skills

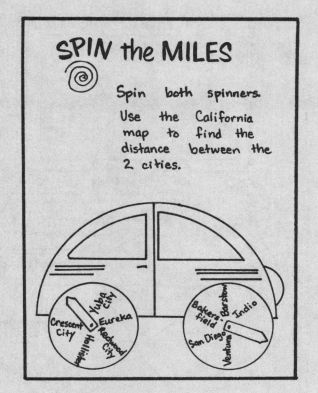

GAMES AND ACTIVITIES

1. Write the names of northern cities on one spinner and southern cities on the other (or use eastern and western cities). Children spin both wheels and measure the distance between the cities shown, using a national or state map hung at the center. Then they record the names of the cities and the distance in miles.

This activity could also be used as a game. Each child or team would have its own map and race to find the distance the fastest.

2. Use graph paper pasted on cardboard to make the game board. Make a set of playing cards, each card stating a direction to move such as one square north.

To play, everyone starts in the middle. In turn each child draws a card and follows the directions. The first to reach any edge of the board wins.

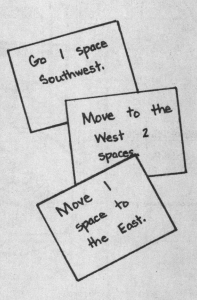

3. Make a set of task cards with questions using information found on the map. Children use a U.S. road map to find the answers and record them in their travel books. Toy cars may be used to actually travel the route.

4. Make a set of cards with the names of maps that might be included in an atlas. A child picks a card and makes that map to add to the atlas.

WORKSHEETS

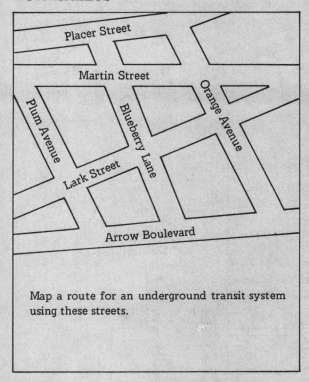

Map a route for an underground transit system using these streets.

What kind of map would you use to find out. . .	
what to wear to visit a new city	
which bus to take	
location of the park	
how people live there	
which mountains are nearby	
which areas have the most people	

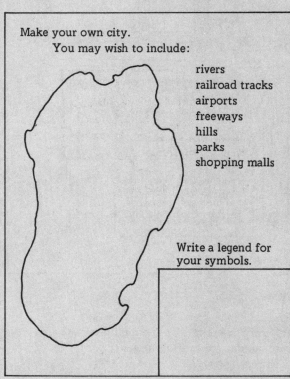

Make your own city.
    You may wish to include:

rivers
railroad tracks
airports
freeways
hills
parks
shopping malls

Write a legend for your symbols.

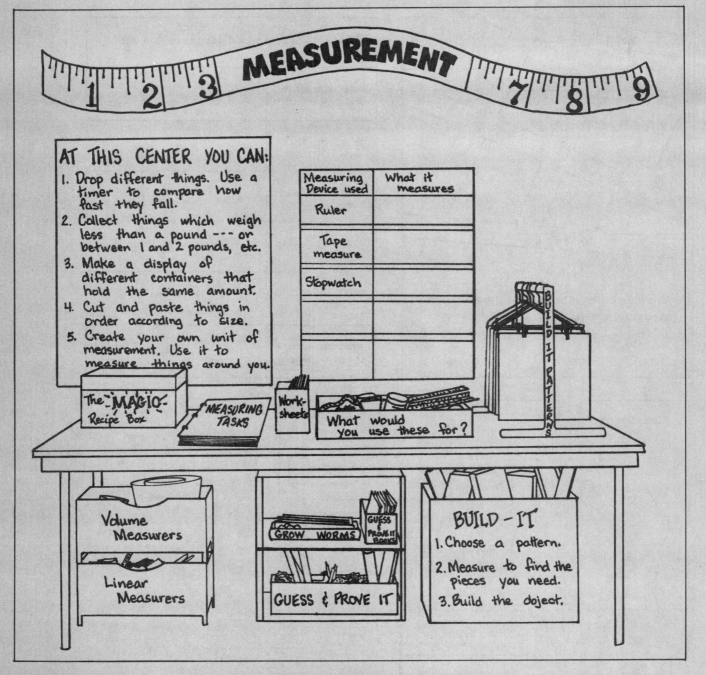

MEASUREMENT

AT THIS CENTER YOU CAN:
1. Drop different things. Use a timer to compare how fast they fall.
2. Collect things which weigh less than a pound --- or between 1 and 2 pounds, etc.
3. Make a display of different containers that hold the same amount.
4. Cut and paste things in order according to size.
5. Create your own unit of measurement. Use it to measure things around you.

Measuring Device used	What it measures
Ruler	
Tape measure	
Stopwatch	

The MAGIC Recipe Box

MEASURING TASKS

Worksheets

What would you use these for?

BUILD IT PATTERNS

Volume Measurers

Linear Measurers

GROW WORMS

GUESS & PROVE IT BOOKS

GUESS & PROVE IT

BUILD - IT
1. Choose a pattern.
2. Measure to find the pieces you need.
3. Build the doject.

Learning Possibilities

Developing the concept of the standard unit of measure
Learning to use different measuring devices appropriately
Using addition, subtraction, and estimation skills
Learning about fractional parts
Learning to follow written directions and diagrams

Make-believe Muffins

1 pt. dirt	1 c. water
1 T. grass	¼ c. sand

Mix ingredients well.
Pour into muffin tins.
Bake in sun until dry.

GAMES AND ACTIVITIES

1. Make recipe cards using ingredients found in nature. Put the ingredients at the center or allow children to get them as they need them.

2. Children measure pieces of pre-cut wood and follow the directions on the card to build the object.

3. Place in a box a variety of measuring tools. Children use them to measure objects and then record their data on the chart.

The MAGIC Recipe Box

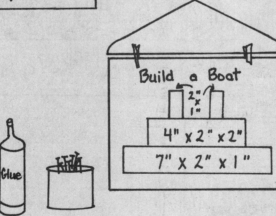

Build a Boat

2"
x
1"

4" x 2" x 2"

7" X 2" x 1"

Glue

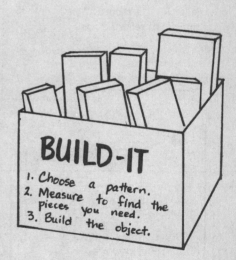

BUILD-IT
1. Choose a pattern.
2. Measure to find the pieces you need.
3. Build the object.

Measuring Device used	What it measures
Ruler	
Tape Measure	

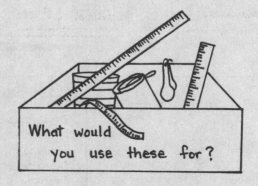

What would you use these for?

4. Get a pair of dice and cover one with fractions. Cut worm heads and seven-inch strips of colored construction paper. Children throw both dice in turn and cut a strip to the length shown on the dice. The first to make a worm 20 inches long is the winner.

5. In a box display objects that are different lengths. Children estimate how long an object is and then measure it. They write their estimations and their measurements in their own record books. Provide an answer book.

6. A task card contains one simply stated problem. Children choose a card, do the task, and record their findings in their own record books.

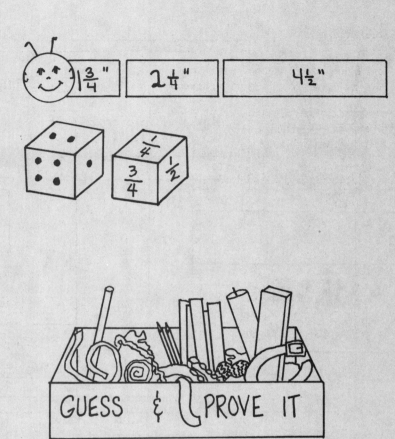

WORKSHEETS

Choose things which can be measured around and up and down.

Measure and show the difference between the height and circumference.

Object	Circumfer-ence (around)	Height (up and down)	Difference

COMPARE & COMBINE

	Most	Least	Make them the same
Weigh			

	Most	Least	Make them the same
Weigh			

	Longest	Make them the same
Measure	Shortest	

	Longest	Make them the same
Measure	Shortest	

MEASURE AND ‹ Enlarge it / Shrink it

Thing measured	As it is	Magnified x 2	Minimized x ½
table top	12" across	24 inches	6 inches

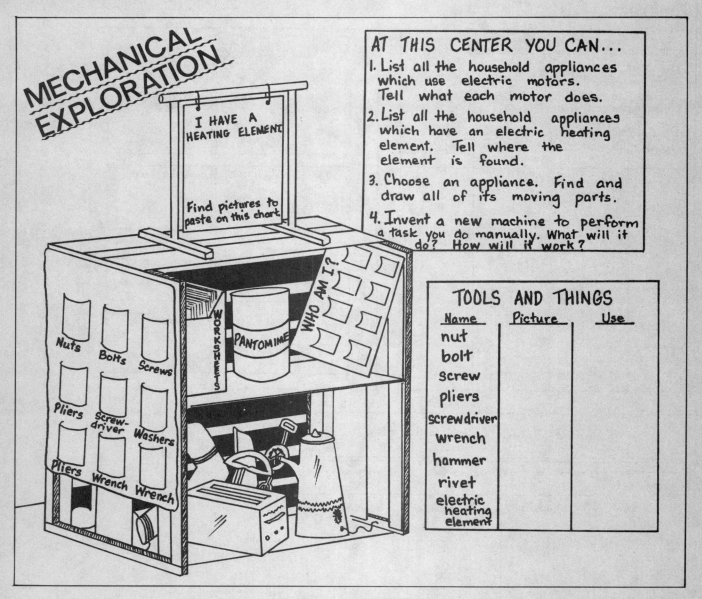

Learning Possibilities

Using simple hand tools

Learning the basic elements common to household appliances and machines

Discovering and exploring how machines work

Center Needs

An assortment of basic hand tools, such as pliers, adjustable wrench, three screw drivers (small, medium, large), needle nose pliers, set of nut drivers, and mallet

A minimum collection of broken household appliances with plugs cut off, and, if possible, various shapes of plumbing pipe

PANTOMIME

1. 1st player picks a card and acts out a tool or appliance for his team.

2. Team has 1 minute to guess which tool it is – a correct guess earns 1 point.

3. After 1 minute, the next team repeats the above steps.

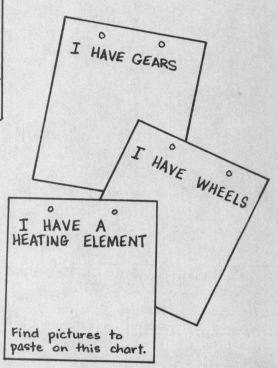

I HAVE GEARS

I HAVE WHEELS

I HAVE A HEATING ELEMENT

Find pictures to paste on this chart.

WHO AM I?

IRON

CARDS

1. Write a description of an appliance on a card and put it in a pocket.

2. Another person will read the card and put the name of the appliance on the pocket.

PLUMBING PIPE

1. Use pipe to construct a duplicate of the pipes under the sink and the drinking fountain outside. Draw or name other things you can duplicate with pipe, such as swings, bannisters, etc.

2. Name the shapes of pipe used in the sink or drinking fountain.

3. Design on the back of this paper something "new" which can be built from pipe.
   What pieces do you need? _____
   How many of each type? _____
   How long? _____
   How will the object be used? _____
   BUILD IT!

FIND MACHINES THAT DO THE SAME KIND OF WORK AS THE TOOL

(For example, a screwdriver turns; what machines turn?)
Cut out or draw pictures to show them.

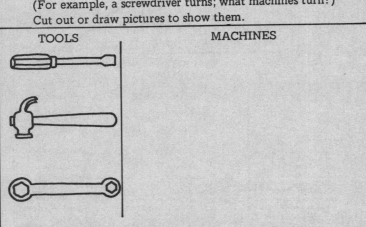

TOOLS	MACHINES

MACHINE TAKE-APART

1. Choose an item to take apart.
   Name it. _____

2. Is it electric? _____ If yes, does it have an electric motor? _____ If yes, tell what the motor does. _____
   _____

3. Does it have an electric heating element? _____
   If yes, where is it and what does it heat? _____
   _____

4. If it's not electric, what makes it work? _____
   _____

5. Draw a design of how the item works.

MYSTERY CENTER

Each mystery you read gives you a ticket to <u>add</u> or <u>build</u> something for our Haunted House.

Tickets

WANTED

WANTED: Crime and detection mysteries

WANTED: Supernatural events mysteries

Make a poster to advertise a mystery.

Hang it under the correct wanted sign.

Mystery Worksheets

Stir up a Mystery

NEWS

MYSTERY BOOKSHELF

FBI File

MYSTERY CHEST

CLUE BOXES
Choose a box.
Write a clue on each side.
Put the solution inside the box.

AT THIS CENTER YOU CAN:

1. Make a clue list from a mystery you have read. See if someone else can solve the mystery.
2. Record some mysterious sounds on the tape recorder.
3. Listen to the mystery sound tape. Write a mystery to go with it.
4. Do research on the ways real detectives solve crimes.

Learning Possibilities

Learning about two main types of mysteries (crime and detection mysteries and supernatural events mysteries)

Learning the elements of a mystery (clues, crime, detection, suspense, excitement)

Stimulating reading and creative writing of mysteries

Using logical thinking in problem-solving activities

GAMES AND ACTIVITIES

1. Let the children develop the ideas for the mystery pot. Write the ideas on colored construction paper, a different color for each category.

2. A collection of objects is placed inside the chest and changed periodically. Students use the objects as clues in writing their own mysteries.

3. This ticket accompanies the Haunted House bulletin board. A child earns a ticket by reading a mystery.

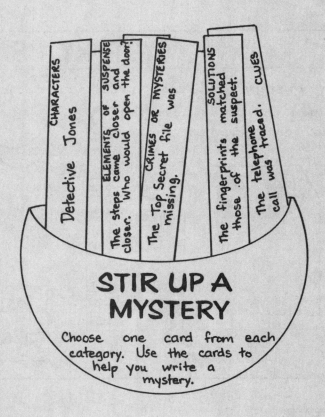

CHARACTERS

Detective Jones

ELEMENTS OF SUSPENSE

The steps came closer and closer. Who would open the door?

CRIMES OR MYSTERIES

The Top Secret file was missing.

SOLUTIONS

The fingerprints matched those of the suspect.

CLUES

The telephone call was traced.

STIR UP A MYSTERY

Choose one card from each category. Use the cards to help you write a mystery.

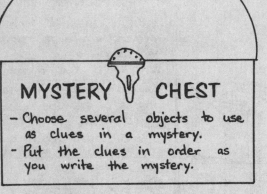

MYSTERY CHEST

- Choose several objects to use as clues in a mystery.
- Put the clues in order as you write the mystery.

This ticket entitles

_____

to work on the.

HAUNTED HOUSE.

A glove was dropped.

The time of the theft was established as about 11 p.m.

MYSTERIOUS DISAPPEARANCE OF BUILDING PLANS

THE MYSTERY OF THE TOP SECRET BUILDING

by Donny

4. Making clue boxes is a means of motivating children to read and share mysteries. The child writes or draws a clue on each section of the outside of the box and puts the solution inside. Children should have easy access to a wide variety of different-sized boxes.

5. A child may cut out the headline of a real-life mystery from the newspaper and use the main idea to write his own mystery book. Books should be bound and placed on the Mystery Book Shelf. This is a good opportunity for children to learn simple book binding techniques.

6. Ditto this form onto 5 x 7 cards, and place the cards in a file box at the center.

F.B.I.   CARD

Book title: _____

Author: _____

Prove it's a mystery. Does it have these elements? Give examples.

EXCITEMENT: _____

CLUES: _____

CRIME: _____

DETECTION: _____

SUSPENSE: _____

Agent Information

Height: _____

Weight: _____

Age: _____

Fingerprint

F.B.I.* FILE

*Famous Book Investigations

Can you solve the mystery of "what is a mystery?"

My book's title: _____

The author: _____

1. What type of mystery is it?
   A. Crime and detection
   B. Supernatural events
2. List the elements in the story which <u>prove</u> that it is a mystery.

A. Excitement _____
   _____

B. Clues _____
   _____

C. Crime or mystery _____

D. Detection _____
   _____

E. Suspense _____
   _____
   _____

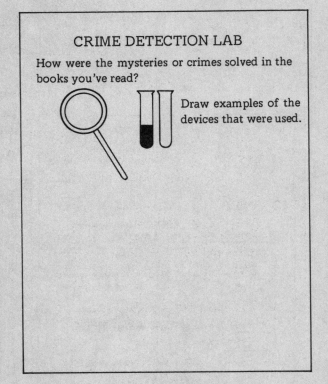

CRIME DETECTION LAB

How were the mysteries or crimes solved in the books you've read?

Draw examples of the devices that were used.

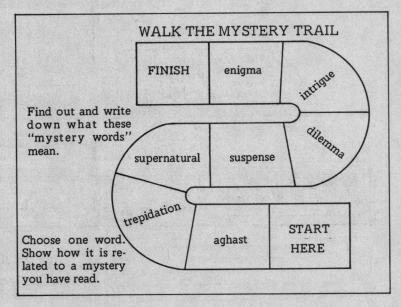

WALK THE MYSTERY TRAIL

FINISH   enigma   intrigue

dilemma

Find out and write down what these "mystery words" mean.

supernatural   suspense

trepidation

aghast   START HERE

Choose one word. Show how it is related to a mystery you have read.

NOW MUSIC

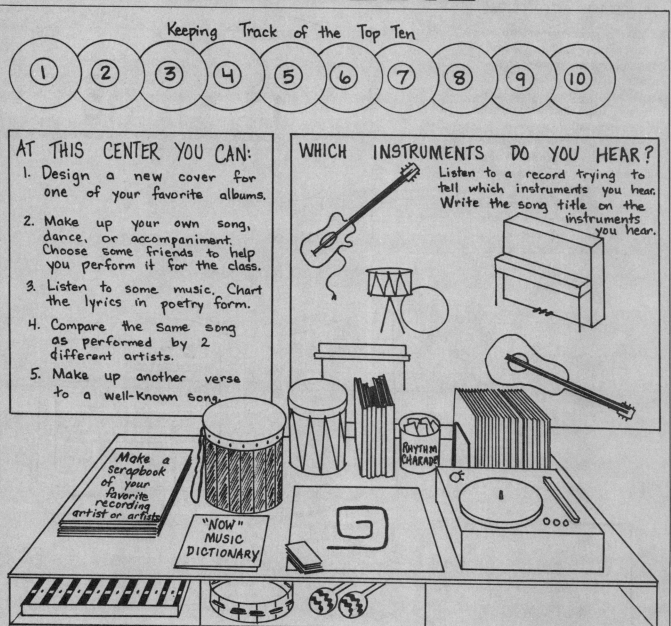

Keeping Track of the Top Ten

1 2 3 4 5 6 7 8 9 10

AT THIS CENTER YOU CAN:

1. Design a new cover for one of your favorite albums.

2. Make up your own song, dance, or accompaniment. Choose some friends to help you perform it for the class.

3. Listen to some music. Chart the lyrics in poetry form.

4. Compare the same song as performed by 2 different artists.

5. Make up another verse to a well-known song.

WHICH INSTRUMENTS DO YOU HEAR?

Listen to a record trying to tell which instruments you hear. Write the song title on the instruments you hear.

Make a scrapbook of your favorite recording artist or artists

"NOW" MUSIC DICTIONARY

RHYTHM CHARADE

Learning Possibilities

Developing listening skills and learning to recognize the sounds of various instruments

Translating current music into its rhythmic component

Stimulating reading and writing about current popular music

Developing dictionary skills

Learning to draw conclusions from survey data

GAMES AND ACTIVITIES

1. Make ten paper records to hang at the center. Children write the top ten songs of the week on them. In selecting the top ten, they may use a radio station list or take a survey of their classmates to make up their own list.

2. Place large construction paper and yarn of various colors at the center for children to use in making scrapbooks. In these scrapbooks children may keep pictures, news-clips, and information about their favorite recording artist or artists.

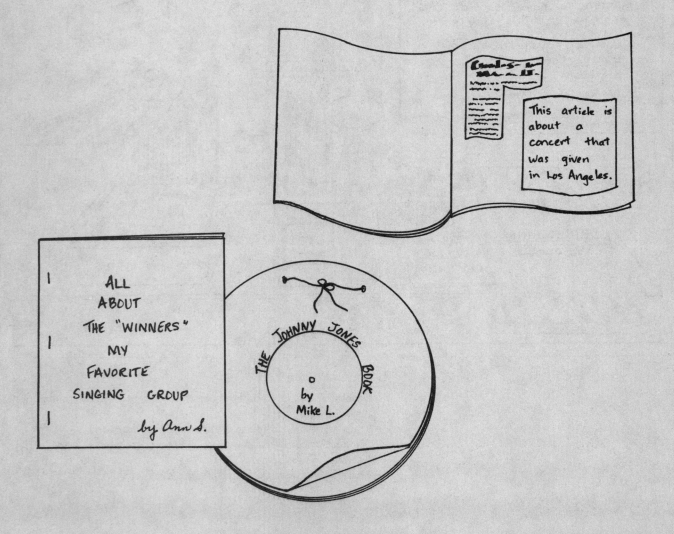

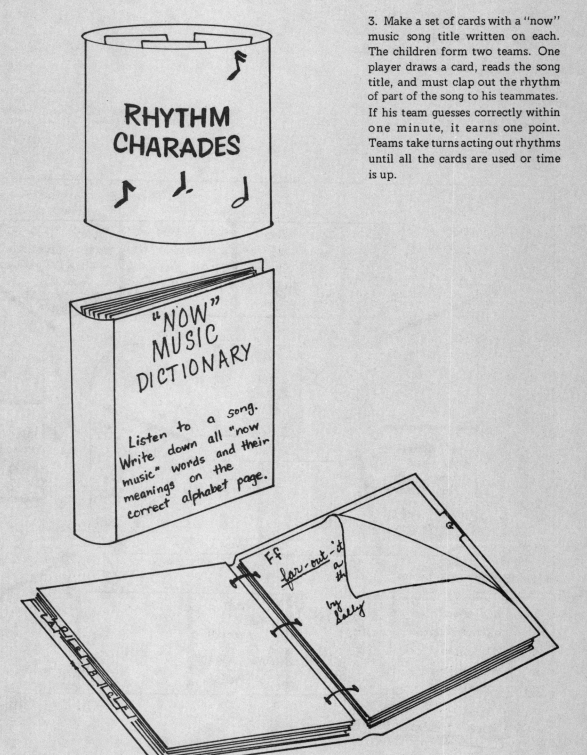

3. Make a set of cards with a "now" music song title written on each. The children form two teams. One player draws a card, reads the song title, and must clap out the rhythm of part of the song to his teammates. If his team guesses correctly within one minute, it earns one point. Teams take turns acting out rhythms until all the cards are used or time is up.

4. Make a set of cards with questions about current recordings, artists, instruments, etc. Write the number of spaces to advance if the answer is correct. Put the answers on the backs of the cards and write directions on the game board which will make the game more exciting.

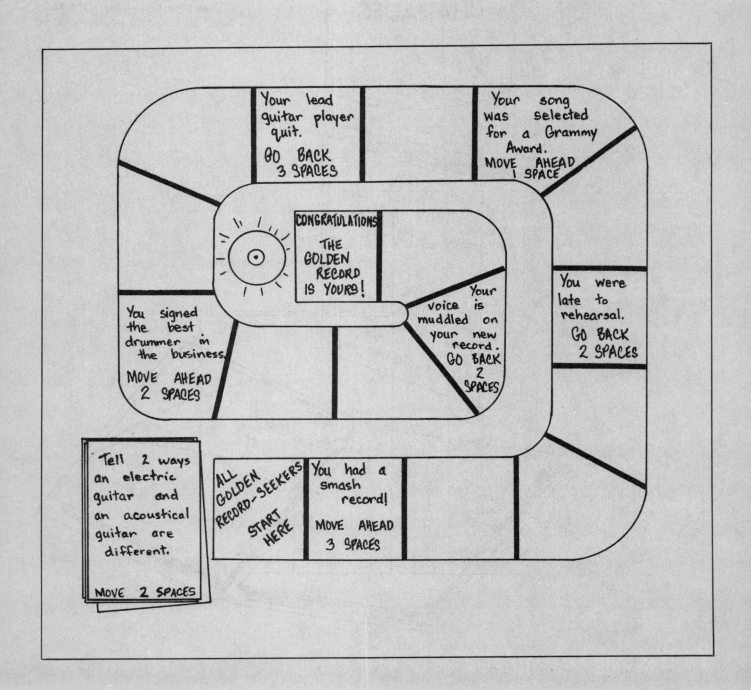

WORKSHEETS

Take a survey of people's favorite songs.
What conclusions can you make based on your survey?

Favorite Song	Age of Person Surveyed	Occupation	Average time spent listening to radio per day

Conclusions:

*Make up another music survey.

Listen to 10 records at home or at school.
Write the song titles on one of the record categories below.

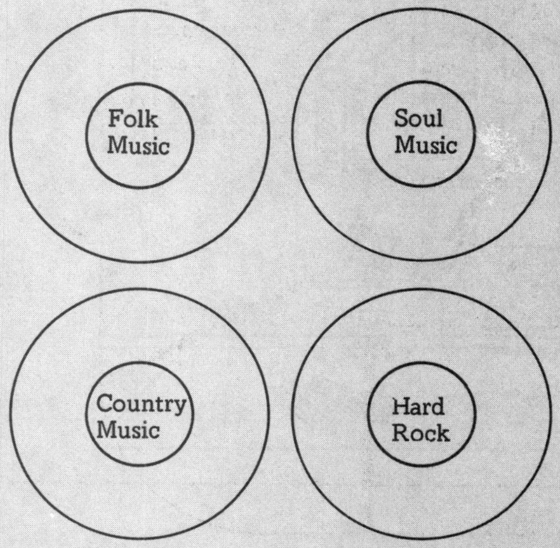

Folk Music

Soul Music

Country Music

Hard Rock

For Dee Jays Only

Plan an hour's listening time for a radio audience.

Record Title	Recording Artist	Playing Time
		Total Time = 60 min.

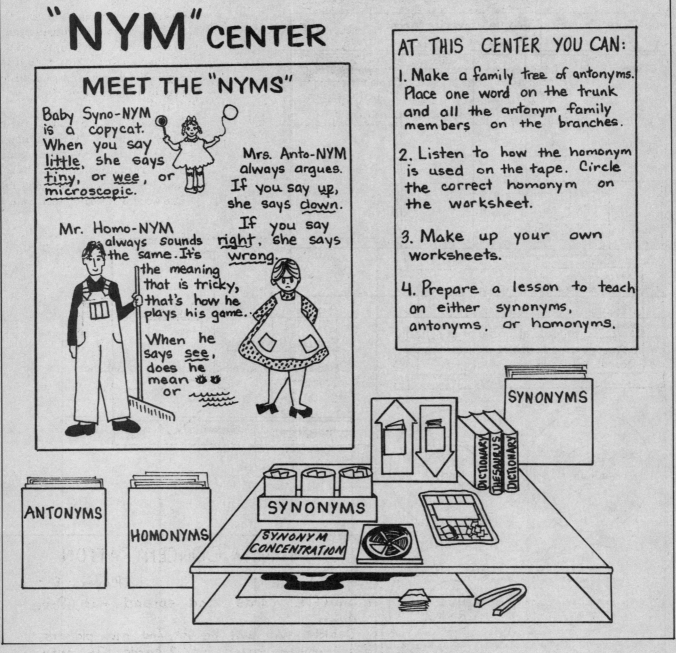

Learning Possibilities

Broadening oral and written vocabulary usage
Recognizing the meaning of synonym, homonym, and antonym
Knowing the appropriate use of synonyms, homonyms, and antonyms
Using dictionaries and thesauri

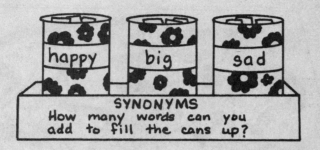

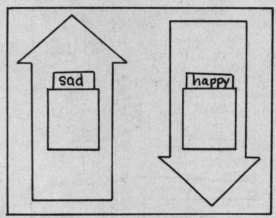

GAMES AND ACTIVITIES

1. Paste a word on each can. Cut small cards to put with the game. Children find a synonym, write it on the card, and drop it into the can. Dictionaries and thesauri are helpful for locating words.

2. Make the game board out of heavy cardboard. Use two library pockets to hold the cards during play. The envelope on the back is filled with pairs of antonym cards. One word is placed on each card.

SYNONYM CONCENTRATION

Directions: Players: 2-4
1. Shuffle cards and spread out face down.
2. Decide who will be 1st, 2nd, etc. players.
3. 1st player turns up 2 cards. If they are synonyms he takes them. If not, he turns them face down again.
4. Each player, in turn, tries to match two synonyms.
5. The game is played until all cards are paired.

3. Write pairs of antonyms on cards, placing one word on each card. Put a paper clip on each card. Children take turns using a magnet to pick up the words which form the antonym pair.

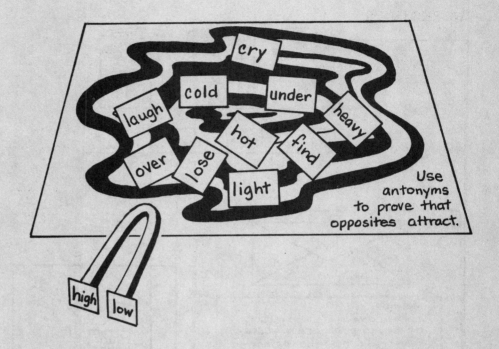

Use antonyms to prove that opposites attract.

ANTONYM-O
Directions: Caller calls words. Players cover the antonyms on their cards. The first player to complete a row is the winner and next caller.

happy	over	high	before
lose	late	ahead	laugh
begin	★ FREE	elastic	hard
cold	success	war	slowly

WORKSHEETS

WRITE a sentence and PICTOGRAPH the homonyms in it.

1. pail
   pale

2. blew
   blue

3. knight   The   went to the
   night   castle at

4. dye
   die

5. flour
   flower

6.

7.

Fill the garden with synonym flowers.
How many can you grow?

REWRITE the story.
Use synonyms to replace the underlined words.

   One day a <u>little</u> boy was <u>walking</u> down the <u>street.</u> He <u>saw</u>
a coin lying on the sidewalk.
   He <u>looked</u> all around but <u>saw</u> no one. So he bent down and
<u>picked up</u> the coin.
   He <u>wanted</u> to <u>find out</u> who it belonged to, so he <u>started</u>
<u>going</u> to the houses nearby.
   Finally, the boy <u>found</u> the person who had <u>lost</u> the coin.
The person <u>gave</u> him a reward for returning the coin.

Now . . . write your own story. Underline the synonyms.
Give it to a friend to replace the underlined words.

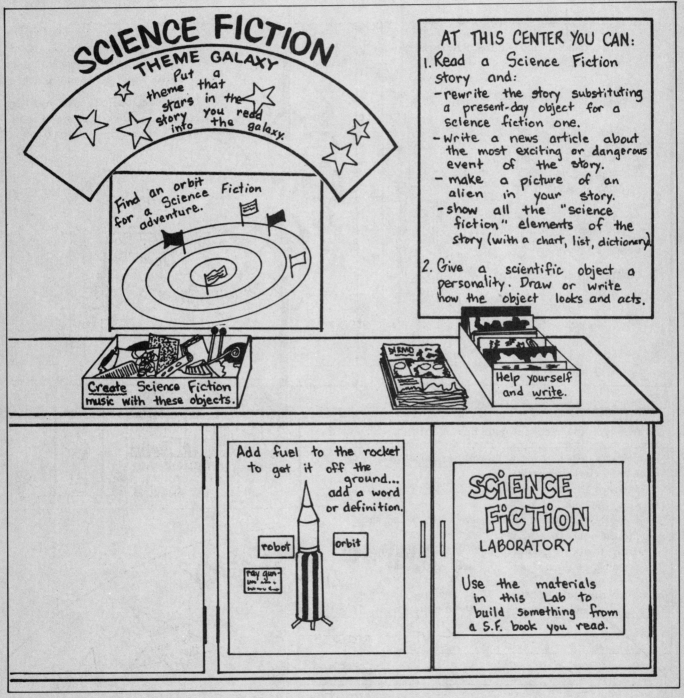

Learning Possibilities

Stimulating reading and creative writing
Recognizing the theme of a story and being able to write from a given theme
Transforming real-life situations into imaginary ones
Categorizing
Matching auditory images to verbal or visual images by creating music

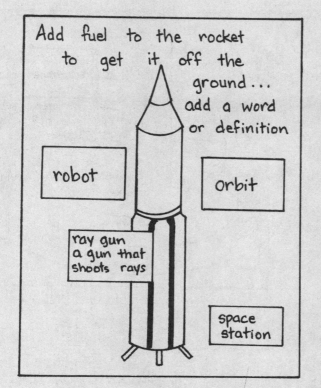

GAMES AND ACTIVITIES

1. Children write science fiction vocabulary (with or without definitions) from their stories on cards and place them on the rocket.

2. Cut comic strips out of the newspaper. Children choose one to rewrite and redraw as science fiction.

3. On flags, children write adventures from their stories and place them in the right orbits.

4. Children use the materials to create their own science fiction music to accompany stories they have read or written.

5. Fill science fiction book jackets with paper. Children write their own science fiction stories using the title or picture as motivation.

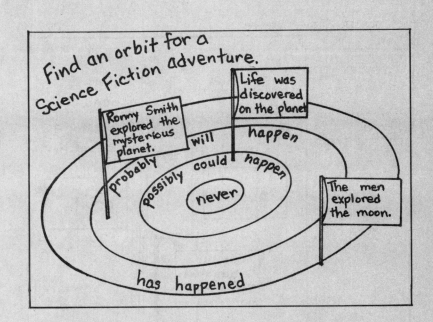

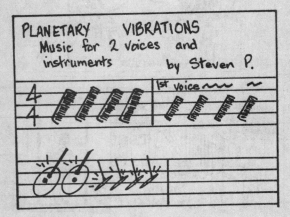

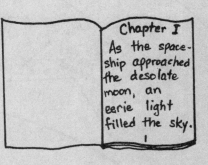

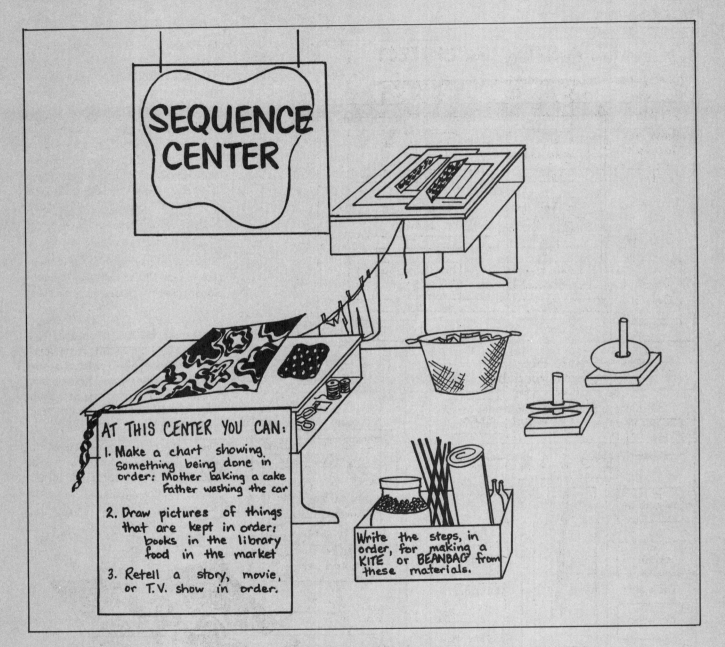

At this center you can:

1. Make a chart showing something being done in order: Mother baking a cake Father washing the car

2. Draw pictures of things that are kept in order: books in the library food in the market

3. Retell a story, movie, or T.V. show in order.

Write the steps, in order, for making a KITE or BEANBAG from these materials.

Learning Possibilities

Learning to sequence words, story parts, events, and directions
Identifying activities that are done in a logical sequence
Developing the skill of retelling stories and events in order
Recognizing that time changes things

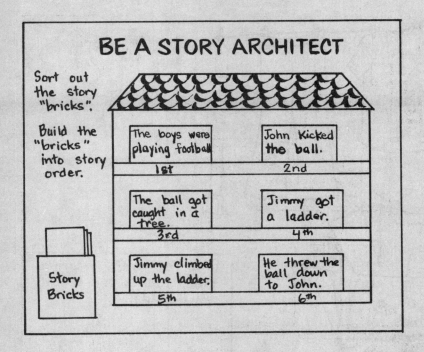

BE A STORY ARCHITECT

Sort out the story "bricks".

Build the "bricks" into story order.

Story Bricks

The boys were playing football	John Kicked the ball.
1st	2nd
The ball got caught in a tree.	Jimmy got a ladder.
3rd	4th
Jimmy climbed up the ladder.	He threw the ball down to John.
5th	6th

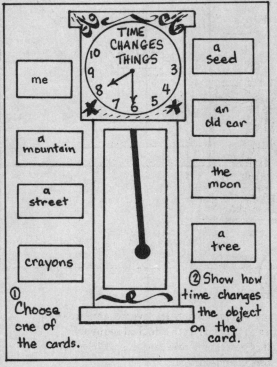

TIME CHANGES THINGS

me
a mountain
a street
crayons

a seed
an old car
the moon
a tree

① Choose one of the cards.

② Show how time changes the object on the card.

Steps in making my beanbag
1. Cut 2 pieces of cloth the same size.
2. Put right sides together. Sew around edges. (over)

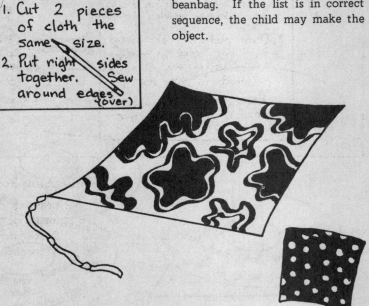

GAMES AND ACTIVITIES

1. Write the parts of a story on 3x5 cards, or cut out a story from an old book and paste it on cards. Number the cards on the back to show the correct sequence.

For a primary student, color code the cards of each story to aid in sorting. For older children, use the same kind of cards for all the stories. In this way part of the process involves finding the parts of a story that go together and putting them in order.

2. Children may write or draw their responses. Change the cards occasionally, letting children suggest new objects.

3. Display materials for making a beanbag and a kite, full size or miniature. Kite: paper, string, material for a tail, frames or toothpicks, glue, scissors, crayons, and paint. Beanbag: cloth, beans, needles, thread, embroidery yarn, and scissors.

On a piece of paper children list the steps necessary to make a kite or beanbag. If the list is in correct sequence, the child may make the object.

4. Cut out sets of clothing (shirt, pants, belt, socks, and hat). On each piece of clothing, write one word from a sentence. Each set of clothing makes a complete sentence.

Children hang the clothes on the line to make a sentence. They then take a clothes ditto, color the outfit in any way they wish, and write the sentence they made at the bottom.

5. Make two identical sets of donut-shaped cards. Write sentences from a short story on the cards, one sentence to a card.

To play, both students look at their story cards and arrange them in the correct sequence. Then they toss them in order on their own posts. The first to finish with the order correct is the winner.

WORKSHEETS

MAKE A SEQUENCE PUZZLE

Draw the main parts of your favorite story in the sections below. Paste this page on cardboard. Cut the sections apart to make a puzzle for others to do. Don't forget to put the answers on the back.

STITCH-A-SENTENCE

1. Number the words in order for a sentence.
2. Use a needle and thread to sew them together into a sentence.

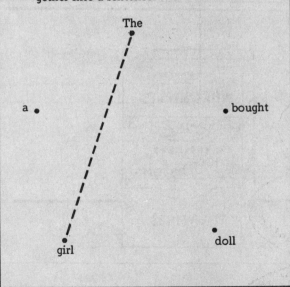

WHAT DID YOU DO?

Keep a log of what you do during two days. How do your days compare?

Time	One Day	Another Day
8:30		
9:00		
10:30		
12:00		
2:00		

Learning Possibilities

    Learning basic set operations
    Learning to use the vocabulary of sets
    Reinforcing counting and one-to-one correspondence
    Developing the ability to categorize and see relationships

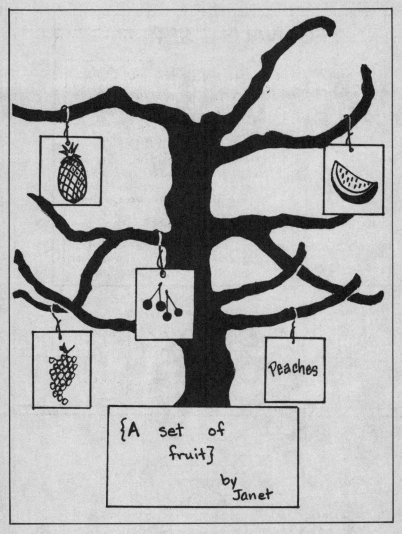

GAMES AND ACTIVITIES

1. Children cut out and paste, draw, or write the members of a set and hang them on the tree with Christmas tree hooks. Then a card is written to describe the set and placed under the tree.

2. The union of sets or other set operations may be shown using embroidery hoops and objects. The teacher and children can provide cutouts of felt, plastic, or paper. Real objects can also be used.

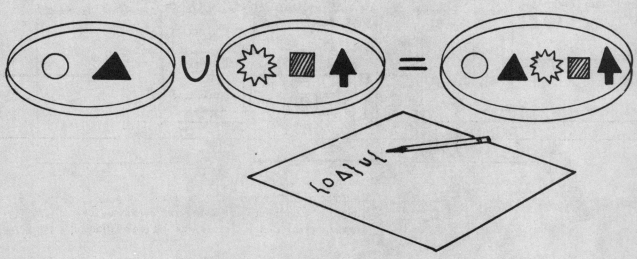

3. Children cut out and paste or draw equivalent sets and describe them at the bottom.

4. The teacher places two notebooks at the center. One is filled with picture and word sets. (These may be made by the children as a beginning set experience). A direction card is placed with the notebooks. It may be changed daily or weekly depending on the aspect of sets being studied.

The children write or draw whatever is called for on the direction card. They tear out their pages and label them with their names and corresponding page numbers.

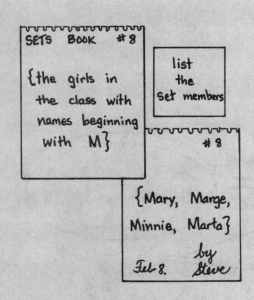

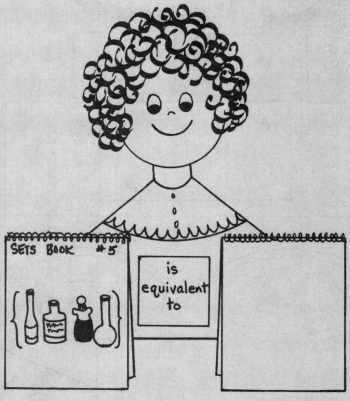

WORKSHEETS

Sub Set Insects

Use the set members on the bodies to write subsets on the insects' legs.

{a, b, c, d, e}

{1, 5, 9, 13, 17, 21}

{the set of red fruit}

{the days of the week}

Join the sets to make a picture.

{fish, dog, cat}   U   {tree, pond}

{girl, boy}   U   {T.V., chair, rug}

Cut and paste the number that matches each set.

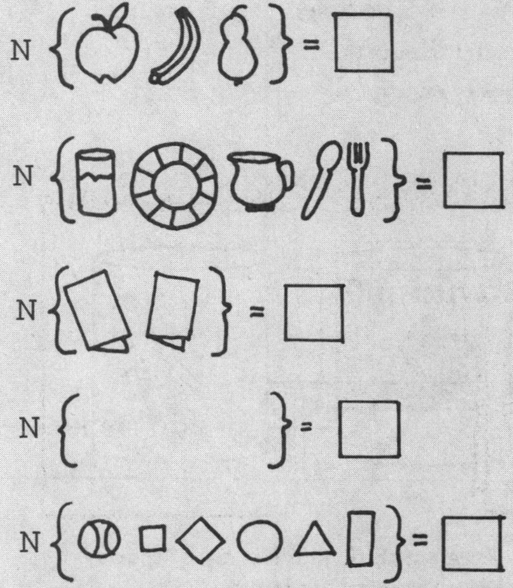

N {🍎 🍌 🍐} = ☐

N {🥛 🍽 ☕ 🍴} = ☐

N { ☐ ☐ } = ☐

N { } = ☐

N {⚾ ☐ ◇ ○ △ ▯} = ☐

| 4 | 6 | 1 | 3 | 0 | 5 | | 2 |

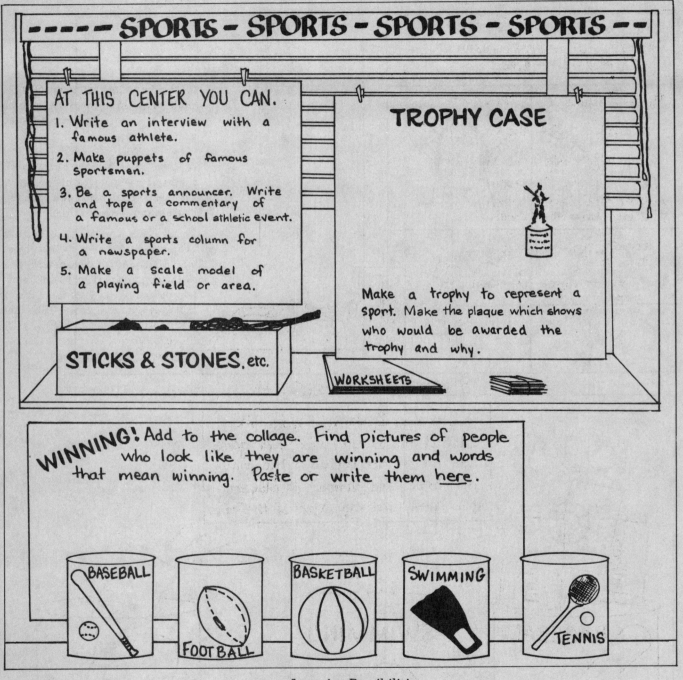

SPORTS - SPORTS - SPORTS - SPORTS

AT THIS CENTER YOU CAN.

1. Write an interview with a famous athlete.
2. Make puppets of famous sportsmen.
3. Be a sports announcer. Write and tape a commentary of a famous or a school athletic event.
4. Write a sports column for a newspaper.
5. Make a scale model of a playing field or area.

STICKS & STONES, etc.

TROPHY CASE

Make a trophy to represent a sport. Make the plaque which shows who would be awarded the trophy and why.

WORKSHEETS

WINNING! Add to the collage. Find pictures of people who look like they are winning and words that mean winning. Paste or write them here.

BASEBALL FOOTBALL BASKETBALL SWIMMING TENNIS

Learning Possibilities

Comparing past and present through the study of sports
Developing the technique of news reporting
Categorizing
Making inferences about people's feelings from their bodily and facial expressions
Using creative thinking to develop original games

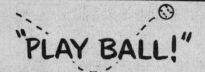

"PLAY BALL!"

Players stand in a line.

The caller holds the cards.

The caller asks the first person to name one fact about the person on the card. If the answer is correct, the player keeps the card.

The player with the most cards wins.

GAMES AND ACTIVITIES

1. Have the children bring their baseball or other sports trading cards to school for this game.

2. In a box place some objects that could be used in a game, such as sticks, a stone, cans, ropes, balls, some chalk, etc.

3. Label ice cream containers with the names of sports. Children write sports words on cards and drop the cards in the correct cartons.

To play as a game, one child stands behind each sports can. The player who is "it" throws a beanbag in one of the containers. The person standing behind it must name a word that goes with that sport. If he can, "it" must throw again. If he can't, he becomes the new "it." The object is to keep from becoming "it."

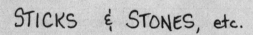

STICKS & STONES, etc.

Choose 2 things from the box and make up your own game. Remember to include the playing area, the number of players, the rules, and the object of the game.

BASEBALL

SWIMMING

FOOTBALL

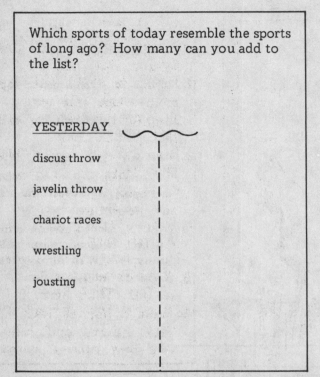

Which sports of today resemble the sports of long ago? How many can you add to the list?

<u>YESTERDAY</u>

discus throw

javelin throw

chariot races

wrestling

jousting

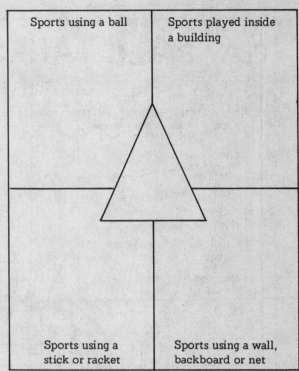

Sports using a ball

Sports played inside a building

Sports using a stick or racket

Sports using a wall, backboard or net

What do you know about these sports?
Use an encyclopedia or other books to see if you can find out more.

Sport	Country	Equipment	Number of Players	Playing Area
La Crosse				
Soccer				
Jai Alai				
Rugby				
Polo				

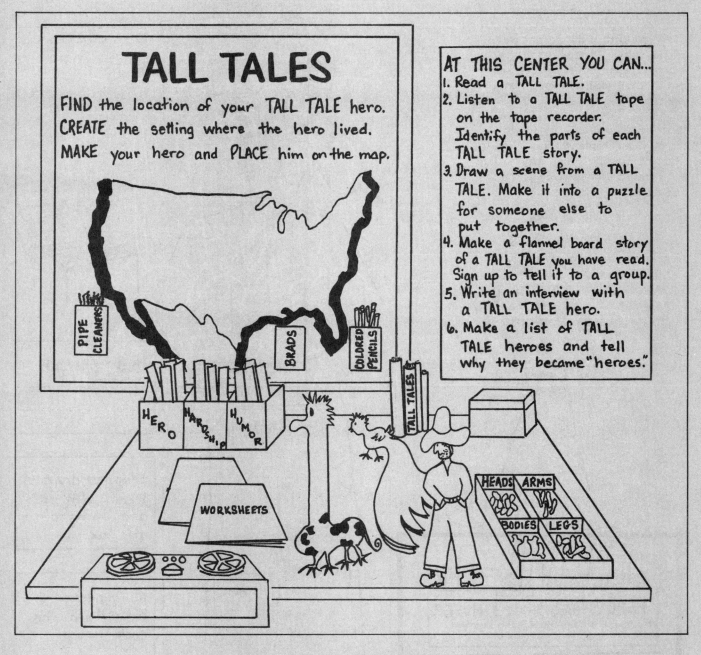

Learning Possibilities

Learning the elements of a tall tale (humor, exaggeration, hardships to overcome, and heroes)

Enjoying and appreciating tall tales

Understanding the contributions of tall tales to American fiction

Relating tall tales to folk tales and American history

GAMES AND ACTIVITIES

1. Make a ditto of the separate parts of the body. Children fill in their story parts, cut out the pieces, and put their tall tale hero together with brads.

2. Items for each category are written on 3 x 5 cards which children read and classify. They may also add items to each category as they read tall tales.

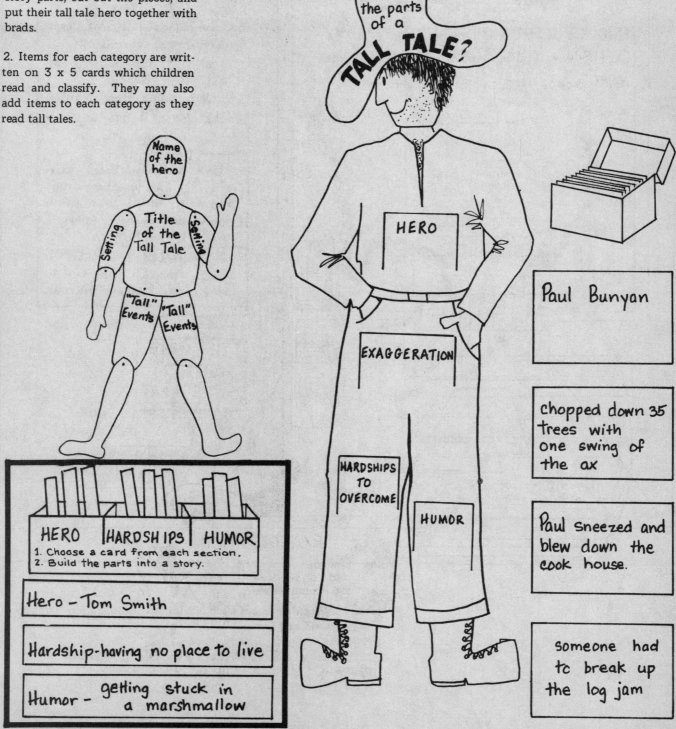

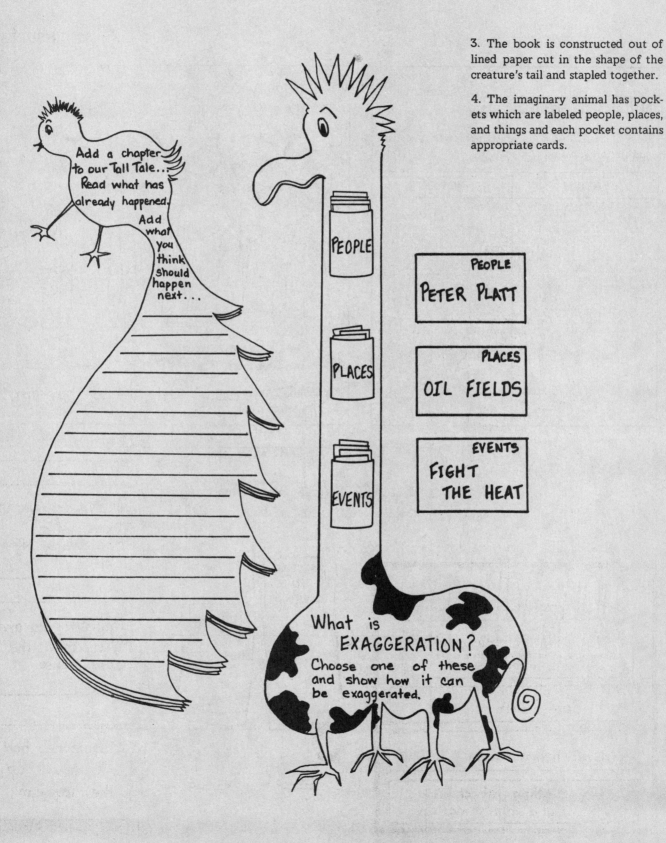

3. The book is constructed out of lined paper cut in the shape of the creature's tail and stapled together.

4. The imaginary animal has pockets which are labeled people, places, and things and each pocket contains appropriate cards.

Add a chapter to our Tall Tale... Read what has already happened. Add what you think should happen next...

PEOPLE

PLACES

EVENTS

PEOPLE
PETER PLATT

PLACES
OIL FIELDS

EVENTS
FIGHT THE HEAT

What is EXAGGERATION? Choose one of these and show how it can be exaggerated.

American fiction TALL TALES contain elements of realism and fiction.

Read a TALL TALE. Give examples of the realism and fiction you find.

REALISM	FICTION

READ A
TALL
TALE

Write the TALL happenings from a TALL TALE on each tree trunk.

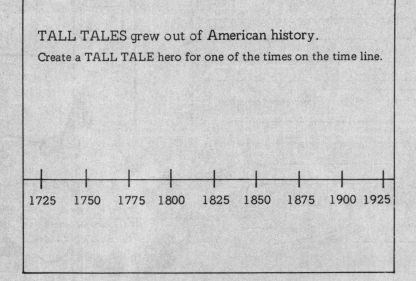

TALL TALES grew out of American history.

Create a TALL TALE hero for one of the times on the time line.

1725   1750   1775   1800   1825   1850   1875   1900   1925

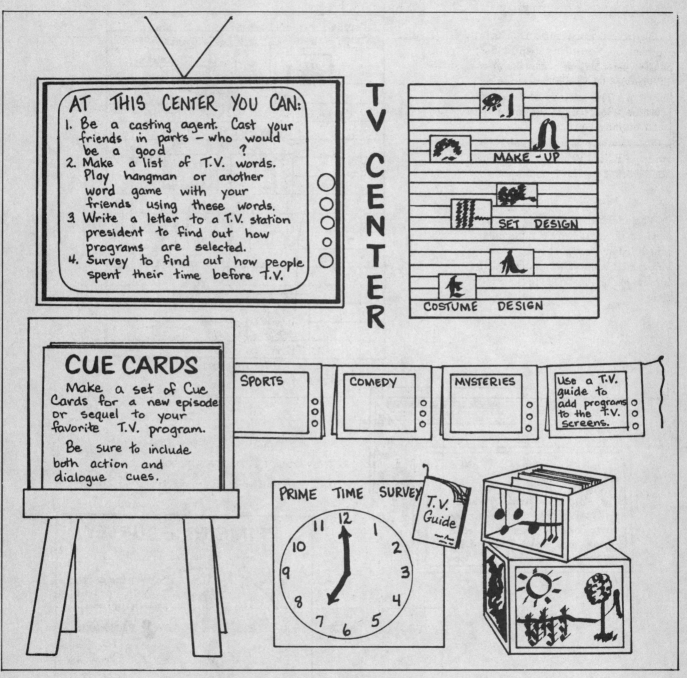

AT THIS CENTER YOU CAN:

1. Be a casting agent. Cast your friends in parts — who would be a good ___?
2. Make a list of T.V. words. Play hangman or another word game with your friends using these words.
3. Write a letter to a T.V. station president to find out how programs are selected.
4. Survey to find out how people spent their time before T.V.

T V CENTER

MAKE - UP

SET DESIGN

COSTUME DESIGN

CUE CARDS

Make a set of Cue Cards for a new episode or sequel to your favorite T.V. program.

Be sure to include both action and dialogue cues.

SPORTS

COMEDY

MYSTERIES

Use a T.V. guide to add programs to the T.V. screens.

PRIME TIME SURVEY

T.V. Guide

Learning Possibilities

Developing the ability to observe details and to reproduce them in another way

Evaluating the effectiveness of advertising

Stimulating reading and writing talents

Using categorizing and surveying techniques

Learning to write time schedules

GAMES AND ACTIVITIES

1. Children may mount their sketches on a sentence strip holder or they can costume and make-up a doll or person rather than making drawings. The set may be designed in a box or in a part of the room.

2. This activity can be done by a group in school or assigned for fun homework for those who want to do it.

3. The children should be encouraged to consider why a program is scheduled at a certain time, for what audience it is intended, and whether it should be changed to another time.

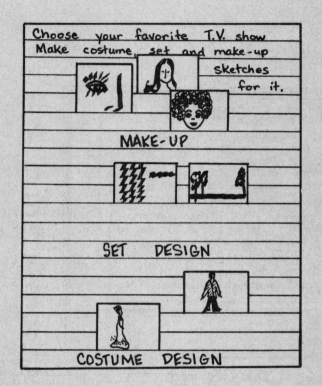

Choose your favorite T.V. show
Make costume, set and make-up sketches for it.

MAKE-UP

SET DESIGN

COSTUME DESIGN

BE A COLOR T.V. EXPERT

Watch a T.V. show in black and white. Transform one scene into color, as it would look on color T.V. Staple your scene to a box.

PRIME TIME SURVEY

Set the clock to a prime time.

Use the T.V. Guide to find all the programs showing at that time.

WORKSHEETS

DOES THE COMMERCIAL SELL?

Product: _____

Who are they trying to sell to? _____
_____

Do you think it's a good product? _____
Why? _____
_____

Would you buy it? _____

Elements of the commercial

_____ Musical jingle   _____ Slogan
_____ Background music   _____ Humor
_____ Well-known personality
_____ Factual information
_____ Other

Design your own commercial here.

Survey people to find out if they like your commercial.

Choose a T.V. program you have seen.

Think of 3 important things that happened in it. Draw or write them on the T.V.s in the order they happened.

①

②

③

COMPARE T.V. SCHEDULES FOR

_____
(date)

My Schedule		_____'s Schedule	
Time	Program	Time	Program

Independent Study
4

WHAT IS INDEPENDENT STUDY?

Defining Independent Study

Independent study is an individualized learning plan which allows the student to process information and create an end product to show what has been learned.

Processing Independent Study Information

Processing information is described as those independent study experiences which the student goes through in order to learn how to learn, such as gathering, applying, translating, and synthesizing information. How the information is processed is more important than the content of the material learned.

The Basics of Independent Study

A successful independent study program is dependent on recognizing and planning for these basic elements:

> student self-selection of what is to be studied
> cooperative teacher-student planning of what will be studied and how it will be shown
> alternative ideas for gathering and processing information
> multiple resources which are readily available
> teacher intervention through formal and informal student-teacher dialogues
> skills integrated with the content area being studied
> time specifically allowed for working and conferencing
> working and storage space
> sharing, feedback, and evaluation opportunities
> student recognition for his "expertise" and finished project

DEVELOPING AN INDEPENDENT STUDY PLAN

> Selecting and delimiting a subject or topic
> Discussing and brainstorming possible sub-areas and questions to explore with the chosen subject or topic
> Formulating key questions or issues to pursue and answer
> Developing a commitment to a plan and a time sequence
> Locating and utilizing multiple resources
> Creating a product from the material learned
> Sharing with classmates the findings from the study
> Evaluating the process and the products from the study and how the time was spent
> Exploring possibilities which could extend the study into new areas of learning

ACTIVITIES TO GUIDE CHILDREN THROUGH INDEPENDENT STUDY

DIRECTION is offered to the student through the use of the independent study guides. They serve as a learning road map to move him through the *thinking* and *doing* steps of independent study. The tasks within the independent study guides take the student to an in-depth level of study and promote productive thinking and processing of information.

ACTIVITIES in the independent study guides provide a range and variety of ways for the student to express information he has gathered. Developed to encourage problem solving and critical thinking, these activities extend beyond the usual type of oral or written reports.

CREATIVITY is reinforced in the independent study guides through activities which stress originality of content and use of materials. High priority is placed on involving the student in the *doing* as a vehicle for gathering and assimilating information.

DECISION MAKING is emphasized in the independent study guides by requiring the student to make a choice about which information is to be included in his activity, and how this activity is to be produced.

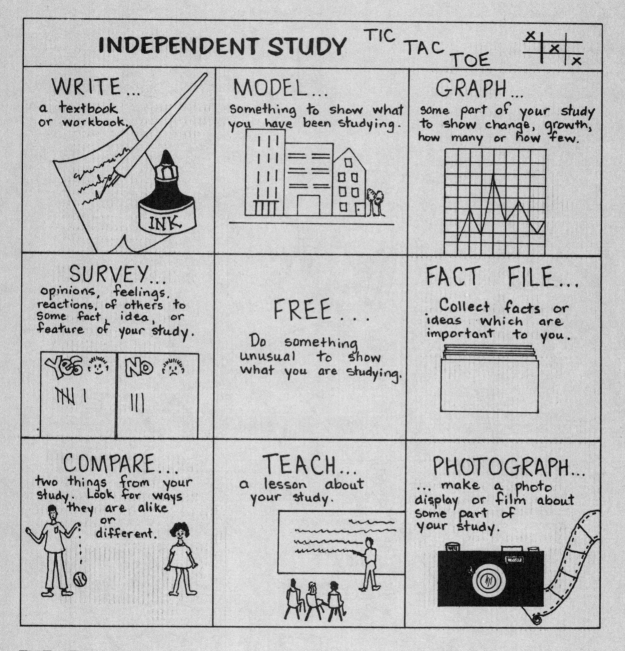

INDEPENDENT STUDY TIC TAC TOE

WRITE...
a textbook or workbook.

MODEL...
Something to show what you have been studying.

GRAPH...
some part of your study to show change, growth, how many or how few.

SURVEY...
opinions, feelings, reactions, of others to some fact, idea, or feature of your study.

FREE...
Do something unusual to show what you are studying.

FACT FILE...
Collect facts or ideas which are important to you.

COMPARE...
two things from your study. Look for ways they are alike or different.

TEACH...
a lesson about your study.

PHOTOGRAPH...
... make a photo display or film about some part of your study.

Tic Tac Toe

Students may tic, tac, toe in any direction doing these activities for their independent study.

Independent Study Wheel

This chart is to be used by students with a self-selected topic. Students are instructed to go through each type of activity around the wheel. Using the wheel allows children to explore different types of activities and levels of thinking.

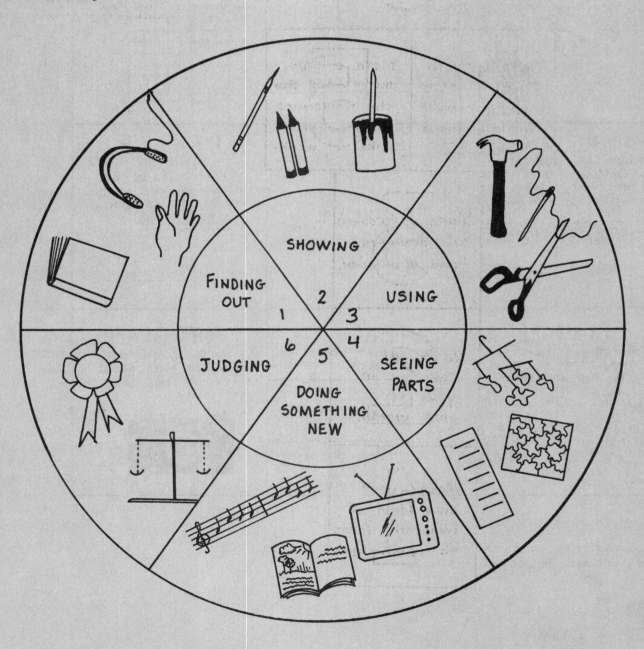

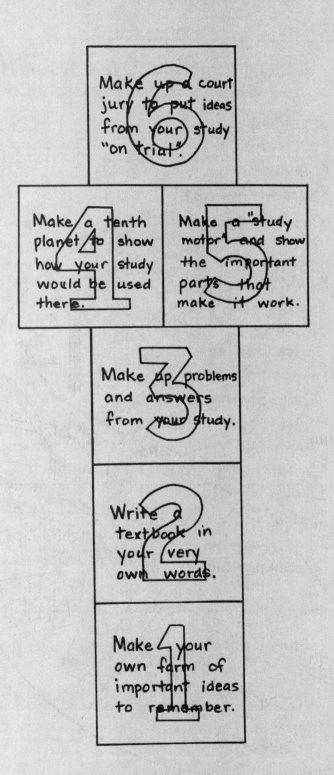

Independent Study Hopscotch

These open-ended activities may be applied to any subject area being studied. The purpose of these activities is to provide new and unusual ways for children to process information. The Hopscotch may be used in numbered sequence or it may be played as a hopscotch game.

Project Alternatives

This independent study guide allows the student to make decisions about the type of skill he wants to perform and the type of product he wants to make. The student matches the verb and the product he has chosen in order to create an independent study activity.

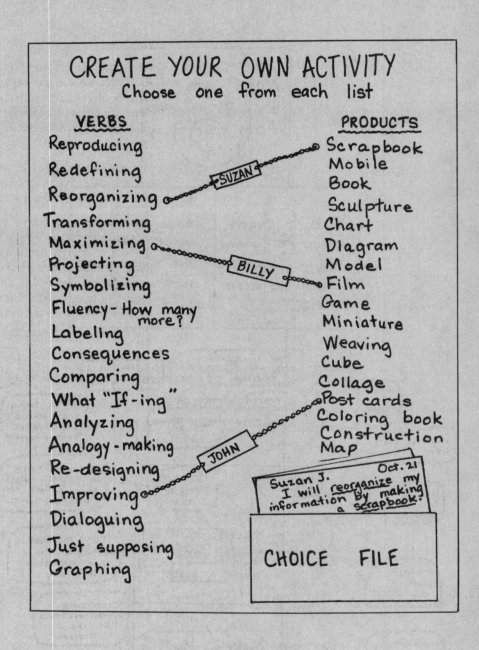

Webbing

Webbing is the process of determining all the possible directions and activities a student can explore as a result of his interest in a specific topic or object. This technique, which expands the teacher's and student's awareness for relating and integrating learnings in a given topic, has been developed and used with great success in the British primary schools.

Through webbing the teacher develops abilities to intervene with the student's learning by asking appropriate questions that stimulate the student to move beyond a narrow consideration of the subject.

The real value of a web is to expand the teacher's thinking about a subject so that there can be spontaneous teacher-student interaction. There is no need to continuously refer to the web, and once the web has been constructed the teacher can begin to think divergently about subjects, and need not go through the formal process with each new topic that is explored in the classroom. Children can be taught to construct their own webs once they understand the intent of the process.

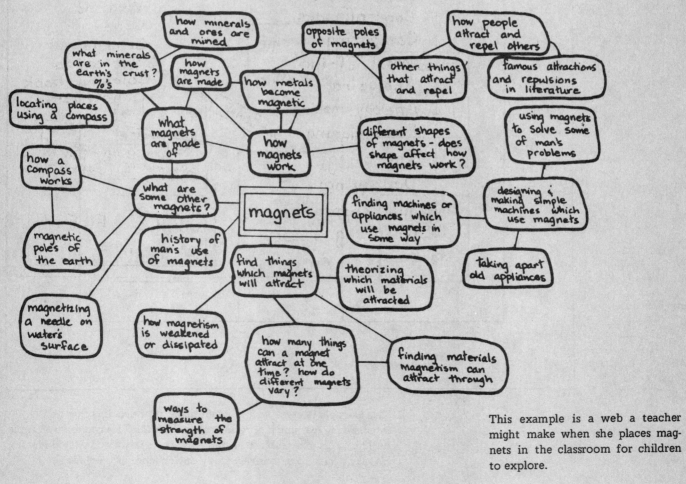

This example is a web a teacher might make when she places magnets in the classroom for children to explore.

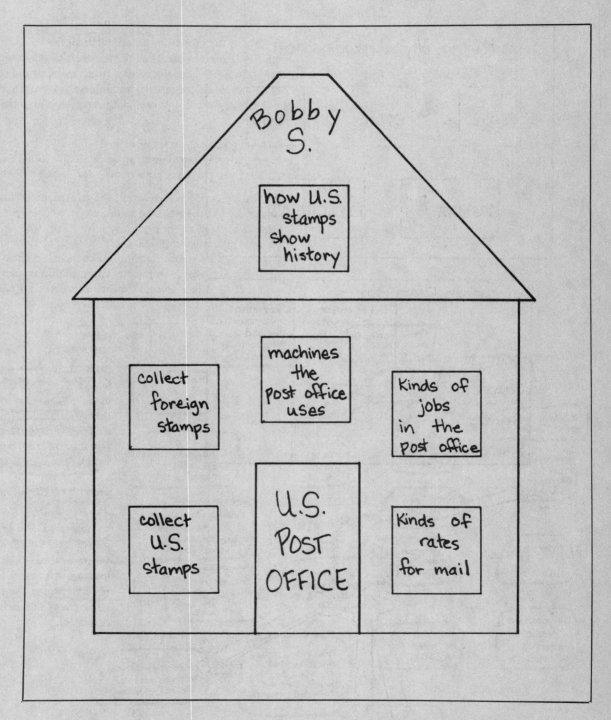

This example is a web a child might make after deciding that he is interested in learning more about the post office. He can draw a simple outline of his main subject of study and write in various related ideas. He may decide to extensively study one or more of these ideas.

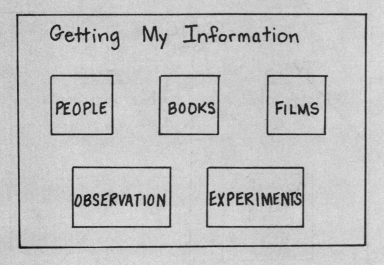

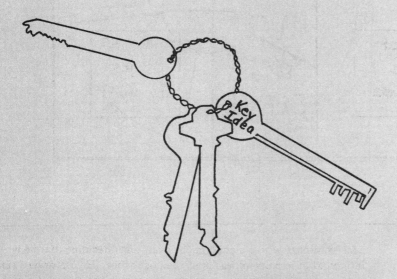

GETTING CHILDREN TO USE MULTIPLE RESOURCES

To help children gather material from many different types of resources, the teacher can direct the students to activities which provide a structure for collecting and classifying information. These activities emphasize locating ideas from a variety of resources and developing *thinking* rather than *copying* skills.

Getting My Information

As data is found, it is placed in the appropriate resource pocket in the chart. Students can sort, outline, and compare the type and content of the information they have found.

Information Chart

Students fill in the sources from which their information was gathered. Then they compare the information found from the various sources by noting likenesses and differences in the concepts or facts which have been collected.

Resource Key Chain

Keys placed on the key chain can be color-coded in order to show the source from which the key idea was taken. For example, red keys could indicate the key ideas taken from observation as a resource, and blue keys could indicate books used as resources.

INDEPENDENT STUDY STARTERS

These organizers provide the initial means by which students can:
    collect information
    record information
    share information
    develop an idea for an independent study project

Their main function is to give some structured guidelines within which students can work independently. Students would work from the basic model and fill in their own subject title and information.

It is a student's choice to determine what information will be recorded and how he will record it—words, phrases, sentences, and/or pictures.

Large pieces of paper and varied raw materials also allow students to be creative within the structure of these independent study organizers.

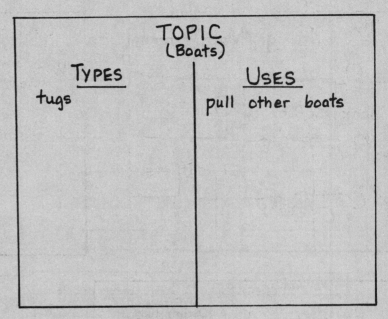

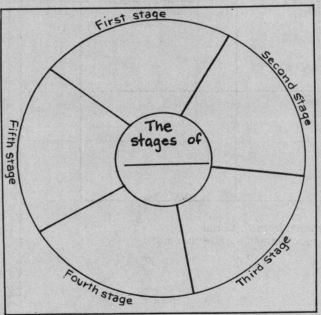

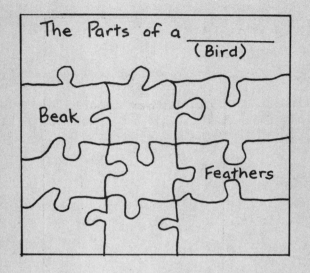

The Parts of a _____
                  (Bird)

Beak

Feathers

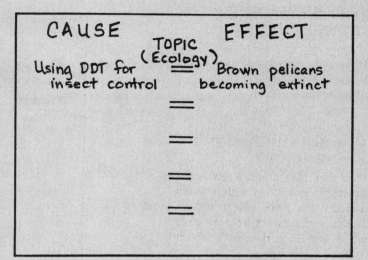

CAUSE   EFFECT

TOPIC
(Ecology)

Using DDT for   Brown pelicans
insect control   becoming extinct

COMPARE

	From study (Heart)	Outside study (Engine)
DIFFERENT		
ALIKE		

Choose one thing from your study.
Compare it to something outside your study.

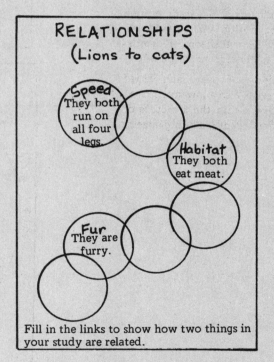

RELATIONSHIPS
(Lions to cats)

Speed
They both run on all four legs.

Habitat
They both eat meat.

Fur
They are furry.

Fill in the links to show how two things in
your study are related.

TEACHER INTERVENTION

Why the Teacher Intervenes

Student-teacher interaction is necessary during independent study. The interaction may be a formally structured conference or a casual conversation as the teacher circulates around the room while the students are working. The teacher intervenes with the student in order to:

keep in touch
help with problem-solving
provide direction
open up new areas for exploration and production
give encouragement
introduce, teach, and/or reinforce a needed skill

Some Questions to be Asked When Intervening

Do you have enough materials?
What do you need?
Are you having trouble finding information?
Do you need help in reading any of the material?
Do you understand the information?
Can you find the information you need in order to answer your question(s)?
How much longer do you think it will take to finish this part of the study?

MAKING PROJECTS FROM RAW MATERIALS

Creative independent study products result when students are allowed to select and manipulate raw materials. Collecting and placing raw materials in a specific location within the room acts as a stimulus for possible independent study products. Students should be encouraged to mix and match materials and use the materials in new and different ways.

Project Cubes

Project cubes are a method of sharing and categorizing processed information and a way to motivate others toward independent study.

Boxes of all shapes and sizes can be used to show the parts of a particular study.

Within one box the student can depict on six sides: subtopics, answers to questions, or concepts learned. With many boxes the student can build a pyramid to illustrate the varying aspects of his study.

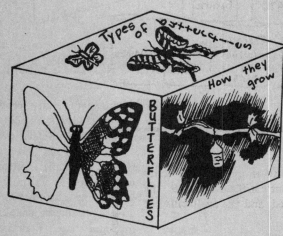

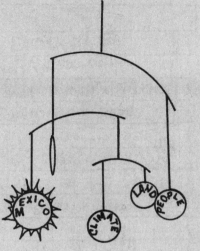

Mobile

Some aspect or concept of the student's independent study can be creatively structured into a mobile art form.

Cans

Each can indicates a sub-area, question, or phase of the student's independent study and becomes a compartment for facts, pictures, and items within that category.

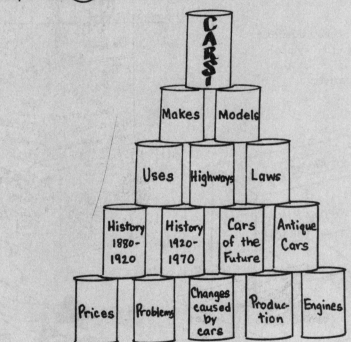

How the information is converted into an independent study product is dependent on the student's artistic interests, the alternatives the teacher has presented, and the availability of raw materials.

Venetian Blinds

Questions and answers from the student's independent study can be exhibited on venetian blinds: questions on one side, answers on the other. Rules can be created which allow other children to use this product as a question/answer game.

Museum

Formed from a box, the museum houses the personal treasures the student has collected or made in relationship to the topic he has studied.

Sculpture

An area or concept of the student's independent study can be symbolized or developed in an abstract form by using scrap materials.

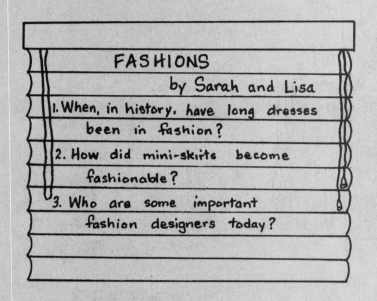

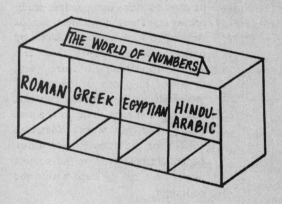

STORING PROJECTS

While students engage in independent study, the amount and types of products in progress can become cumbersome. Storage containers can be created which save space while still making the projects ac-

Sacks

A collection of all types of shopping bags can become storage containers. Hung on hooks, knobs, backs of chairs, coat racks, or hangers, these receptacles are transportable and conveniently kept so that students can easily store their independent study materials.

Ice Cream Containers

Five gallon ice cream containers can be used to store independent study projects. These containers can be stacked to form a set of cubicles by punching holes through them and then securing them with string, yarn, or wire. They can also be stacked separately so that children can pick them up and take them to the area where they will work. Materials needed for the study (books, notes, paper, etc.), as well as the project in progress, can be kept within the container.

RECORD KEEPING

The purpose of independent study record-keeping devices is to encourage student responsibility while keeping the teacher apprised of what the student has been doing.

Contract

Contracts such as these provide a teacher-student agreement within a given time limit.

The expectations for the study are clearly defined by the student with the assistance of the teacher. The contract represents a commitment for a course of action.

Log

This log assists the student in planning and following through on his independent study. It also may serve to help the student evaluate his progress.

~CONTRACT~

_____ with _____
(Student)   (teacher)

SUBJECT:_____

CONTRACTUAL CONDITIONS

What I want to find out:	How I will show what I learned:

DUE DATE:_____
CONSEQUENCES:_____

NAME:_____ DUE DATE:_____

Planning Date: _____

Subject of my study:_____

What I want to find out:_____

Evaluation: _____

Signed: _____   _____
         (student)   (teacher)

KEEPING TRACK OF MY INDEPENDENT STUDY

LOG OF MY INDEPENDENT STUDY			
Date	Accomplishments	Evaluation	Next step (Plans)

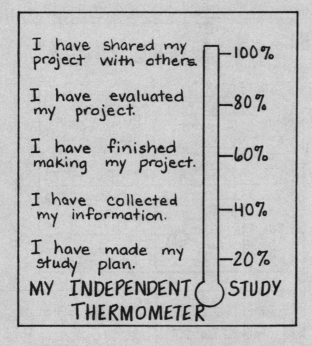

Individual Thermometer

Each student records the progress of his independent study as he moves through the various activities listed on the thermometer.

Group Thermometer

The five thermometers on the bulletin board indicate major activities each student is expected to complete. As a student finishes the activity, he computes the class percentage on the corresponding thermometer.

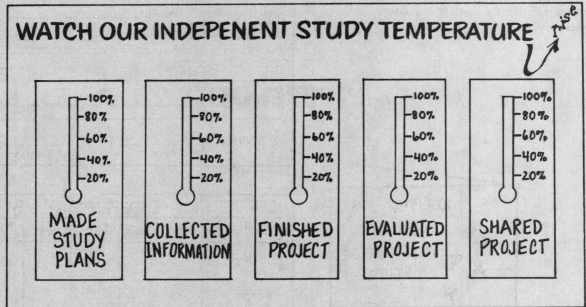

Group Ladder

Each rung of the ladder indicates an activity the learner must do in sequence as part of the independent study program. The student moves his marker as he completes each step of the independent study program.

Individual Ladder

One bulletin board can be set aside for independent study record keeping. Each student's ladder represents an outline of the student's study plan as well as his progress in completing the plan.

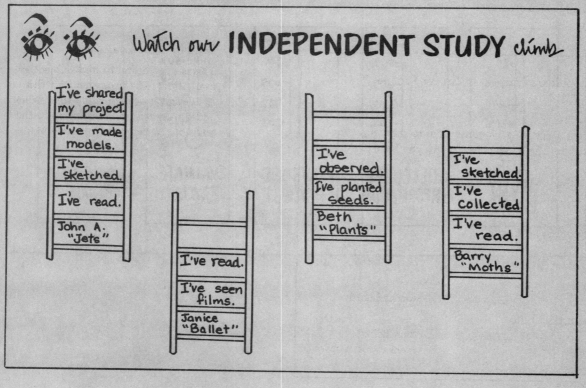

EVALUATIONS

Teacher-Student Conferences

Teacher-student conferences are scheduled or informal meetings where the student shows what he has done and explains why he has done it. Emphasis is placed on the student's learning to evaluate his own independent study project.

Key Questions the Teacher Might Discuss With the Student

What do you like best about the project you are doing (or have completed)? Why?

What parts of your project caused you difficulties? How did you solve these problems?

What new skills did you learn while working on the project (such as typing, lettering, outlining, etc.)?

What sources of information did you use? Did all the sources agree?

Was your independent study plan reasonable as far as goals and time allotment were concerned? How might your plan have been changed? How could other students use your project?

How did you collect or keep track of your information while you were studying? Can you think of another method to use?

What new ideas for another study did you get from the one you have just finished?

Do you have any unanswered questions about your subject? How might you find the answers?

How could you challenge or interest others to study your subject?

Student Self-Evaluation

This is a self-administered, subjective evaluation. The instrument for this evaluation is developed by the teacher and the student in relationship to the goals of the independent study plan.

Example: Independent Study Profile

Name _____ Subject _____ Date _____

Directions: Place a check on each continuum to show how you feel about the independent study you have completed.

1. Use of Resources
   many _____ few
   same _____ different

2. Finished Project (or Product)
   ordinary _____ unlike any others
   written _____ constructed

3. Use of Time
   wasted _____ worked hard

4. Feelings About the Study
   satisfied _____ dissatisfied
   learned enough _____ need to learn more

Class Sharing

The student is given an opportunity to orally present the end-product of his independent study to the class. Class members respond with questions and/or comments which may clarify or challenge the student's learnings. "The Key Questions the Teacher Might Discuss With the Student," as listed under *Teacher-Student Conferences,* might also be used in this situation. The group should develop standards which serve as a reference as they share and discuss their independent studies.

Independent Study Committee

This committee is made up of from six to eight classmates chosen by the students and the teacher. The standards for evaluation and discussion of the student's independent study are developed by the group. The evaluation of the independent study is a composite of the group's reaction to it.

Example of Committee Standards for Independent Study Evaluation

Did the student try to use many sources for his information?
Did he conference with the teacher when he needed help?
Did he try to share his information in new and unusual ways?
Was he able to summarize what he learned?
_____
_____

Planning Classroom Time
5

GETTING THE STUDENT INTO MOTION

Planning devices may help students to determine:

WHAT? the activity they select from the alternatives available to them

WHEN? the sequence of the activities they will do within a period or block of time

HOW? the means they will use to perform the activities they have chosen

WHERE? the place they will work

Any or all of these points may be incorporated into a planning device.

The purpose of any planning device is to provide the student with a tool that will help him become an independent and responsible learner and increase his awareness of his abilities and interests. The use of any planning device should enable the student to develop a self-directedness which can be applied in and out of the classroom.

Planning devices provide students with formats that assist them in budgeting their time, programming their learnings, and making decisions from the choice of activities available to them. The type of schedule used depends on the teacher's intent and the students' needs and capabilities. All of the devices offer students a range of choices.

Rotational Scheduling

Groups of children are rotated to learning activities. In this type of scheduling, students do not decide when they will go to the activity or center, but rather what they will do when they get to that activity or center.

Assignments

Children are assigned to activities or centers according to diagnosed needs. They may choose *when* to go to the assigned area and/or *what* to do at the assigned area.

Contracting

Students develop an agreement which states their choices of what to do, when to do it, and how to do it.

Self-programming

Students are given freedom to set their own course of learning from those activities available in the environment. The teacher may initially allow only the independent students to program themselves while she works with others who are more dependent on teacher direction. The students may move from programming themselves for a small portion of each day to programming themselves for the entire day. The goal is for each student to find his own way to best use his time.

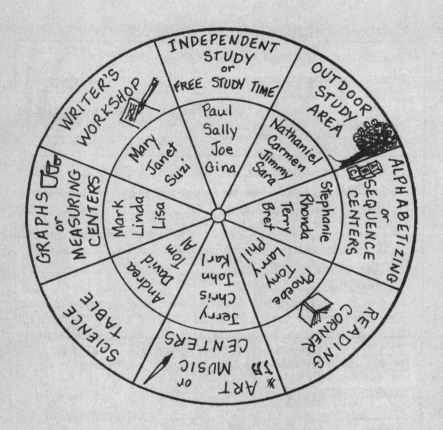

THE STUDENT'S DAY

Circle Planning

The experiences which the teacher thinks are imperative for students are written on the outer circle. The teacher controls the sequence of places where students work by rotating the inner circle during the day, or she can change it at the beginning of each day and instruct the students to do each activity by moving clockwise.

Trail Planning

Each trail represents a sequence of learning activities. Students can be assigned to a trail, or they can select one. This method of planning assures that all students will work at all the areas.

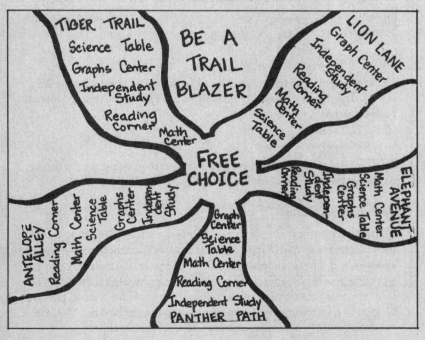

Postcard

The teacher and students can design their own postcards. These act as personalized communications between the teacher and the student. They inform the student of the tasks that have been assigned to him. The student returns the postcards to relate his accomplishments.

Cut and Past Schedule

Assignments for the total class are written in some of the geometric shapes on the ditto by the teacher. The extra shapes are filled in by the teacher and/or student for individualized assignments. When the student completes an assignment, he cuts out the shape on which the assignment was written and pastes it on the other side of the ditto.

Contract Date: _____

I agree to complete the following work by _____
(Date)

_____
_____
Room 2 Official Seal _____
_____
_____

Student's Signature _____

Teacher's Signature _____

MY PLANS

Paul W.

	MONDAY	TUESDAY	WEDNESDAY	THURSDAY	FRIDAY
	Opening / Planning time				
9:15-9:45	ASSEMBLY			Film	
9:45-10:15	ASSEMBLY				
10:15	RECESS				
10:30-11:30		Visit Library		Neighborhood Walk	
11:30	LUNCH				
12:30-1:30	Animal Stories Group	Tall Tales Group	Animal Stories Group	Tall Tales Group	
1:30	PHYSICAL EDUCATION				
2:00-2:30					Film
2:30	EVALUATION / CLEAN-UP				

Schedule O.K'd _____ student initials _____ teacher initials

Learning Contract

Students contract with the teacher to get involved in a learning experience or to perform a specific task. This contract should be developed cooperatively and the terms must be clearly understood by the student. Before signing the contract, he must know the time allotted to complete the work and the consequences if he fails to fulfill the contract.

My Plans

The plans made for the total class are dittoed. The open time blocks are filled in by the student. The schedule is considered to be a contractual agreement when it is initialed by both the teacher and the student. The student's initials signify his commitment to fulfill his plans. The teacher's initials signify her approval of the student's program.

Floor Plan

A diagram or model of the classroom is made. Each student places his flag on the area where he has chosen to work. This method of planning presents the students with an overview of all the learning possibilities which are available to them within the room. It also aids the teacher in keeping track of where students are working at a given time. The diagram can be charted and placed on a bulletin board, or it can be outlined with paint or masking tape on the classroom floor.

Must Planning

The teacher can control learning by presenting students with certain requirements for which they are responsible. Students write their own plans around the outside of the "musts." Each student is expected to schedule his time to include the "musts." But the student decides when to do them.

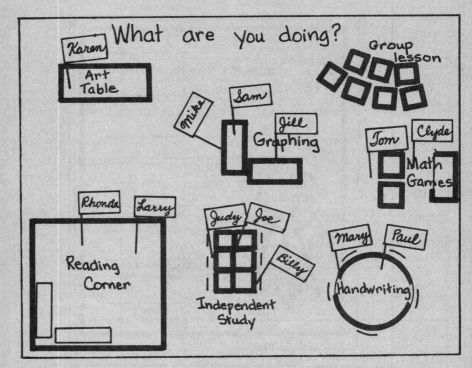

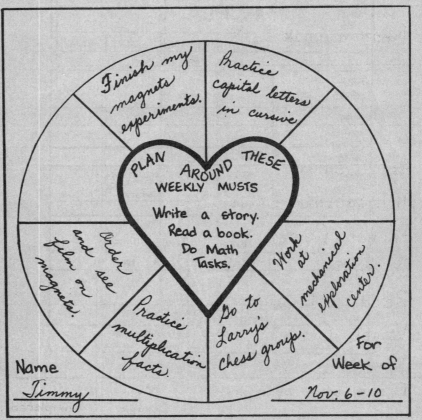

My Plans Name_____	
Write a book	
Games	
Project	
Records, tapes	
Filmstrips	
Flashcards be w see	
Read a book	

	My Choice	I Completed
Art Center		
Alphabetizing Center		
Animal Center		
Go to the Library		
Read a book		
Vowel Center		
Write a story		
I can plan by myself. Name:		

My Plans

Children select and number the activities in the order they will do them. Planning sheets which use pictures help primary students to make learning choices.

Planning Checklist

This planning sheet is designed to schedule children for a particular subject area and block of time. Listed are the learning choices for an individualized language arts program. The student checks where he is going to work. After completing the activity, the student places an X alongside of his choice.

THE TEACHER'S DAY

Who needs my help?

What skills or subjects need to be taught?

What must I do to motivate interest in a center or subject?

The teacher's answers to these questions will determine how he structures his day, interacting with groups and individuals. His daily routine must allow time for teaching, and for engaging in dialogue and intervention with students. For efficient planning and scheduling the teacher must competently assess the class needs and assign priorities for his time on the basis of these needs.

The teacher's schedule should always be a flexible outline of activities. Leaving empty blocks of time allows the teacher freedom to work with students as their needs arise.

Chart Planning

A teacher may use a large spiral tablet to communicate with students, informing the class of what will be done at various times during the school day. This method allows the teacher flexibility in planning each day according to the students changing needs.

Slot Planning

Students record their needs and interests on cards. These cards are placed into slots which have been labeled for different subject or activity areas. The teacher surveys the cards at the end of each day or week and uses them as a reference in planning time and activities for the class.

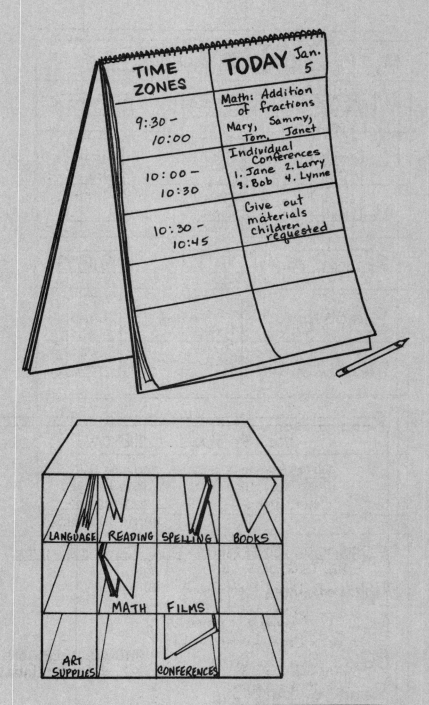

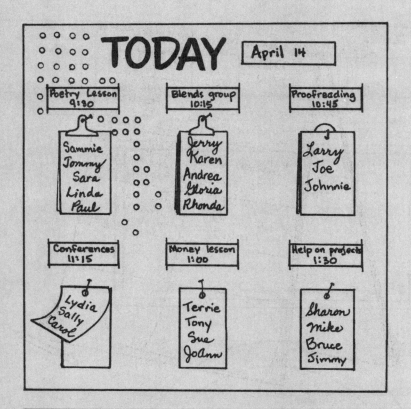

Today

Pads of paper clipped or hooked onto pieces of wood or cardboard form charts which can be used to announce the teacher's schedule for the day. Activity and time headings are written on slips of paper which are slipped into pre-cut slots above each pad. Students sign up for the activities on the pads of paper.

Chalkboard

The teacher fills in the chalkboard outline with the class at the beginning of the school day. This type of planning is a quick and efficient method of indicating what the teacher has planned for certain students. It is also a way of communicating the learning possibilities available to the class.

PLANNING FOR WORK OUTSIDE THE CLASSROOM AND SPECIAL EVENTS

Cup Hook Rack

A rack made of cup hooks inserted into a piece of lumber can be used to keep track of students who are working in areas outside the classroom. Students hang their name cards below the label of the place where they can be found.

Chalkboard

A small chalkboard is placed near a classroom door. Children sign out before leaving the room by writing their names and the areas to which they are going.

Clock Out

Each student is expected to record his name and the place where he will be working on a slip of paper. This is placed in the chart opposite the time he is leaving the room.

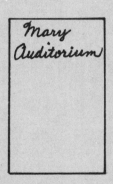

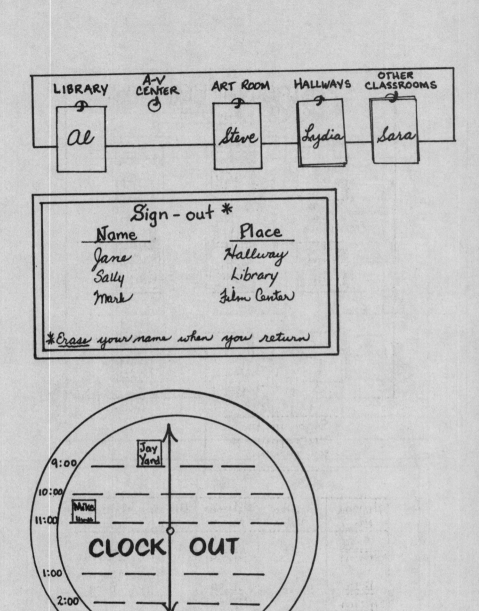

Special Happenings

Advertising special events is a means of introducing and motivating students to current happenings available to them. A sign is clipped over a pocket to announce the activity being presented. The students who wish to participate in the event sign up on strips of paper which they place in the correctly labeled pocket on the chart. This process stimulates student involvement and commitment for the activity. The number of students who can be part of the event can also be regulated.

Acetate Overlay

The use of acetate or plastic over a master weekly schedule enables the teacher to reuse the chart each week. With crayon or grease pencil, the special events for the week are recorded for the students.

Monday May 1	Tuesday May 2	Wednesday May 3	Thursday May 4	Friday May 5
9:30 -Sewing		9:30 -Sewing		9:30 -Sewing
10:00 -African Slides -Bird Walk	11:00 Map Making	10:00 -African Slides		- Rhythm Band

Record Keeping
6

THE IMPORTANCE OF RECORD KEEPING

PARENT: "How is Tommy's schoolwork?"
STUDENT: "What have I been learning?"
TEACHER: "How will I know what each child is doing?"
PRINCIPAL: "Mr. Jones, how are you accounting for your students'
               learning?"

Record keeping is a continuous process which involves the student and the teacher in accounting and reporting individual growth and learning progress. The devices used for record keeping indicate which tasks the student has undertaken and how much he has accomplished. While records show what the student has done, they also help in planning for future learnings.

The teacher and the student share the responsibilities for maintaining the records. They also decide which record-keeping instruments and procedures to employ.

Record keeping cannot be separated from evaluation. Whereas record keeping tells what has been accomplished, evaluation tells how well it has been accomplished.

For the Parent: Records form a comprehensive picture of the student's activities in the classroom.

For the Student: Record keeping develops the child's responsibility for charting and following through on a course of study. It provides the child with a feeling of accomplishment and an identity as a learner. The record-keeping process also helps students to see many possibilities for learning.

For the Teacher: Records supply the teacher with a permanent accounting of what the student has been doing, and thus allows the teacher to further plan and provide for the student. Records are a reference for interpreting pupil progress to parents.

RECORD KEEPING FOR CONFERENCES

Anecdotal Records Notebook

This notebook can be used by the teacher for recording information gathered in conferences and from observations. Records can be used to plan skill groups, report to parents, and show ongoing progress during the year.

Conference Record

This is a method of recording each child's conferences with the teacher throughout the year. Any code may be developed to meet a teacher's needs. The circled letters indicate conferences that have already been held. The empty circles indicate conferences the teacher or child plan to have. At a glance, the teacher can see children she has not conferenced with recently. The record sheet can act as a reminder for writing anecdotal records at the end of the day or week.

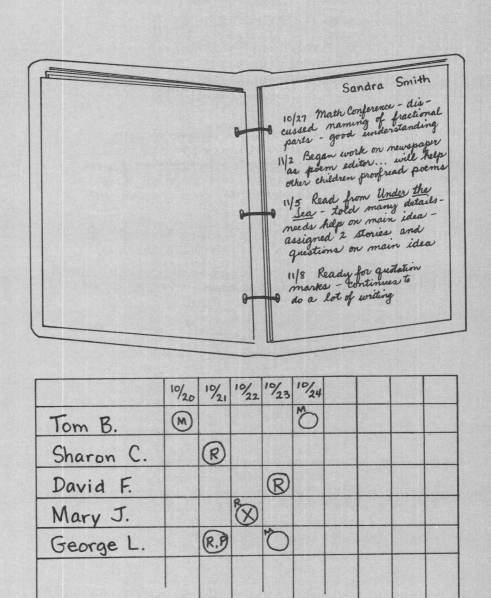

Sandra Smith

10/27 Math Conference - discussed naming of fractional parts - good understanding

11/2 Began work on newspaper as poem editor... will help other children proofread poems

11/5 Read from *Under the Sea* - told many details - needs help on main idea - assigned 2 stories and questions on main idea

11/8 Ready for quotation marks - continues to do a lot of writing

	10/20	10/21	10/22	10/23	10/24			
Tom B.	Ⓜ				ᴹ◯			
Sharon C.		Ⓡ						
David F.				Ⓡ				
Mary J.			ᴿⓍ					
George L.		Ⓡ,Ⓟ		ᴹ◯				

Ⓜ = Math Conference held

Ⓟ = Proofreading Conference held

Ⓡ = Reading Conference held

ᴹ◯ = indicates Math Conference is needed circle is "X'd" when Conference is completed

RECORD KEEPING
FOR READING

My Library and
What Have You Read?

Either page may be used by individual children as a personal reading record. These records may be kept in a notebook, a file box, or a pocket chart at the reading center, or each child may keep his own sheet or card in his reading or work folder. These pages provide a basis of information to help the teacher schedule small group instruction according to needs and interests.

Reading Circles

The teacher identifies the skill areas the students will learn and the activities they will do. Coloring over a part of each circle indicates what the student has accomplished.

Record Garden

A paper cup, a pipe cleaner and colored paper are used to construct the garden. The skill the student is working on is printed on a piece of paper which becomes the center for a flower. The activities which the student has done to learn the skill are written on paper also. These become petals for the flower, and they are glued to the pipe cleaner stem. Students can make a different garden for each skill they are learning, or they can add another flower to the same garden.

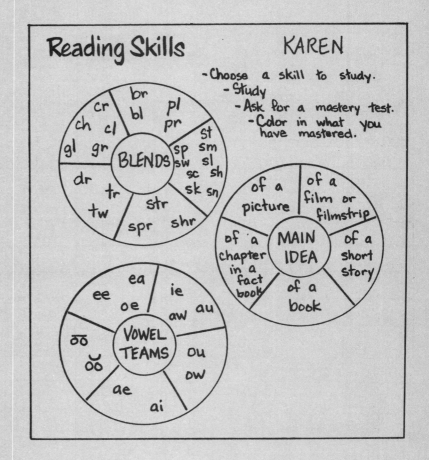

I KNOW...					
the basic addition facts					
the basic subtraction facts					
the basic multiplication facts					
the basic division facts					
I CAN...					
add without regrouping					
add with regrouping					
add columns of numbers					
subtract without regrouping					
subtract with regrouping					

RECORD KEEPING FOR MATH

Individual Record

Each child has a card. The cards for the class may be kept in a three-ring notebook or in a filebox at the math center, or each child may keep his own in his math folder. The child records the date of the test or conference when mastery of the skill is achieved.

Total Class Record

This chart, showing the dates mastery was achieved in various skills, is kept by the teacher. At a glance, the teacher can see the need for specific skill groups and the children who should be in the group. For example, Mary, Karen, and Tommy might be part of a group to learn addition with regrouping. Both charts can be used to keep records of the computational skills mastered.

	Add without regrouping	Add with regrouping	Column addition	
JOHN A.	9/27	9/30	10/30	
MARY	9/30	10/7		
BETH	9/30		9/30	
STAN D.	9/30	10/30	11/30	
TOMMY	9/30			
KAREN	9/30		10/15	

Apron

The teacher or student writes what the student will be learning on an index card and it is filed in the appropriately labeled pocket of the apron. When the skill is learned, the child moves the card to the other pocket, thereby feeling a sense of accomplishment. This also helps to differentiate what a child needs to learn from what he has already learned. Each child can design his own apron and they can be hung on hangers from a chart rack or classroom clothesline.

Balloon

Each child writes the skill he will be studying on a balloon and colors it yellow. He recolors the balloon with a red crayon when he has mastered the skill. An orange balloon signifies that the child has learned that skill and is ready to tackle a new one.

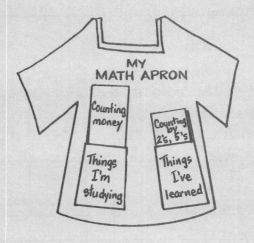

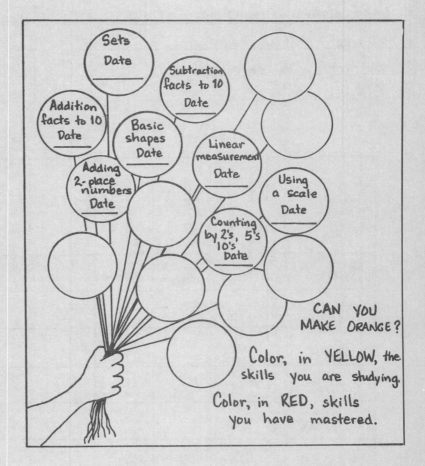

MY SPELL-A-STORY
FOR NOVEMBER
Once upon a time
there was a LONELY
little girl. She lived
on a high WINDY
hill, in a HUGE CASTLE

STUDENTS	SPELLING PATTERNS						
	short vowels	silent e	endings	double consonants	suffixes, prefixes		
Paul							
Jean							
Sally L.							
Jerry							

RECORD KEEPING FOR SPELLING

Spelling Scroll

The student shows that he has learned a spelling word by using it in his monthly story. The scroll keeps track of words learned and shows the student's ability to use words in their proper context. A comparison of monthly stories will provide evidence of the student's progress in spelling and writing.

Spelling Patterns

This record-keeping instrument focuses on the structural rules related to learning how to spell. The teacher fills in the headings after determining the rules which are most appropriate for her class. A check next to a student's name indicates that he has learned to apply the rule.

Spelling Assessment Sheet

This instrument helps the teacher determine each student's ability to apply spelling skills, to learn new words, and to use spelling words in written context. The teacher assesses each student according to subjective and objective methods.

Spelling Box

Each pupil maintains a spelling box to keep track of the words he is studying and the words he has learned. The words in the section labeled "Words I Know" can be used as a source for developing a review spelling list. Students can exchange words to form their new spelling lists.

SPELLING / VOCABULARY DEVELOPMENT			
Needs basic words often	Asks for new words	Looks up own words	Attempts to spell phonetically

Name **Dolores**

Date 4-10	Skill being studied periods	Activity	Written Work Story	Mastery test on 4-18

Activity — Cut and paste / Writing / Mastery

MY Writing Sampler

Date: 2-17-71
Skill: even spacing

1st sample

O | The magic flower grew until it reached the roof-tops

Improved sample

The rocket ship had a silvery, shiny look. It was!

RECORD KEEPING FOR LANGUAGE

Cut and Paste

A student cuts the symbol which indicates his level of progress from the bottom of the page. The symbol is pasted into the appropriate column on the ditto and the activity and date are entered.

Writing Sampler

The teacher and the student define the skill that needs to be developed from the student's own writing. A sample which shows the deficient skill is cut and pasted onto a page in the sampler. A sample showing the student's progress is later cut and pasted on the same page.

Language Study Box

The teacher surveys basic curriculum or class interests and abilities to determine the language areas to be emphasized. These areas become headings for the dividers in the record-keeping box. Each child has a card or cards which identifies his learning need(s) and his progress. The card(s) are filed behind the subject area in which he is working.

My Writing Book

Each student has his own writing book which contains all of his writings. It helps the teacher and student to diagnose the student's needs, and is a continuous record of communication between the teacher and the student.

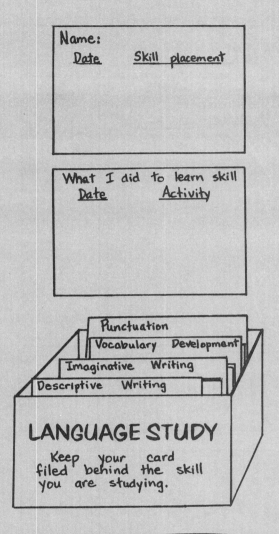

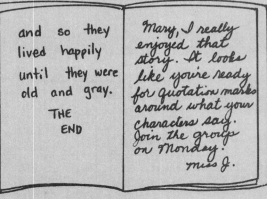

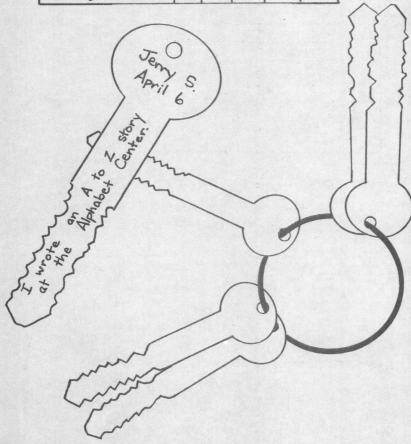

NAME ✔ CHECKING UP ON WHAT I'VE DONE	WEEK OF				
✻ daily "musts"	MON.	TUES.	WED.	THURS.	FRI.
✻ Math Activity					
Independent Study					
Story or poem writing					
✻ Reading					
Handwriting					
Art or Music					
✻ Measurement or Cooking Center					
Animal Stories or Magnets Center					

Jerry S.
April 6

I wrote an A to Z story at the Alphabet Center.

RECORD KEEPING FOR THE WHOLE DAY

Checking Up

Students are required to do the daily musts which have been filled in by the teacher. They complete the rest of their weekly schedule according to their own choices. Students then check off what they have done.

Key Chain

A different colored key is designated for each working area. After working in an area the student fills out a key and adds it to his key chain. In this way he keeps a record of what he did during the day or week. Adding keys to his key chain gives the student a sense of accomplishment and enables the teacher to see how he utilized his time.

Evaluation

7

LOOKING AT LEARNING OUTCOMES

Since the basic purpose of the evaluation process is to enable the student to perceive his progress in relation to his abilities, evaluation itself is more important than the method that is used. The emphasis is on self-evaluation.

"What have you done?" "How well have you done it?" "How do you feel about what you have done?" These are the questions which students are most frequently asked during the evaluation process.

Evaluation must be an integral part of the instructional program and the school day. The teacher's responsibility is to plan the method and time for evaluation and to teach the students how to evaluate. The type of evaluation used is dependent on the student and the learning activity, and may be either oral or written.

Evaluating Academic Growth

The evaluation tool designed for measuring cognitive or academic growth may ask for either a subjective or an objective response. The student's progress may be recorded intermittently or consistently over a period of time.

Evaluating Personal Growth

The basic tool for this type of evaluation is primarily the subjective type which allows the student to express his feelings freely. The student's attitudes about school and his work are included in this affective type of evaluation. Evaluation of the student's self-concept helps him to answer, "Who am I?"

EVALUATION CONFERENCE

The evaluation method which provides the greatest opportunity for student-teacher interaction is the evaluation conference. It is structured to give the student a chance to share his accomplishments and his feelings concerning them. This time is spent in dialogue which allows *both* the teacher and the student to ask and respond to questions and concerns. The student may be asked to demonstrate his newly acquired skills or knowledge. The most beneficial means of evaluating such student progress is to ask the student to apply his learnings in a new or different context. The key to a successful evaluation conference is to provide enough time to *share, discuss,* and *react.* An evaluation conference implies shared leadership and responsibility between the student and the teacher.

Conference Musts

    Designating a conference period or block of time
    Designing a method for children to sign up for a conference time
    Determining a place for the conference
    Deciding the standards which other students in the class must follow while the teacher is conferencing
    Indicating to the students what is to be brought to the conference
    Reminding children to prepare questions they wish to ask.

SELF-EVALUATIONS OF ACADEMIC AND SOCIAL GROWTH

Measuring Up

This self-evaluation tool may be used by the student for assessing any or all learning experiences. A time designated for evaluating reinforces the importance of doing this type of activity.

Diary

Students may keep a diary to record their feelings about a particular learning activity or about the experiences of the entire school day.

HOW DO I MEASURE UP?

Date: _____

What I did:

_____
_____
_____
_____

How I felt about what I did:

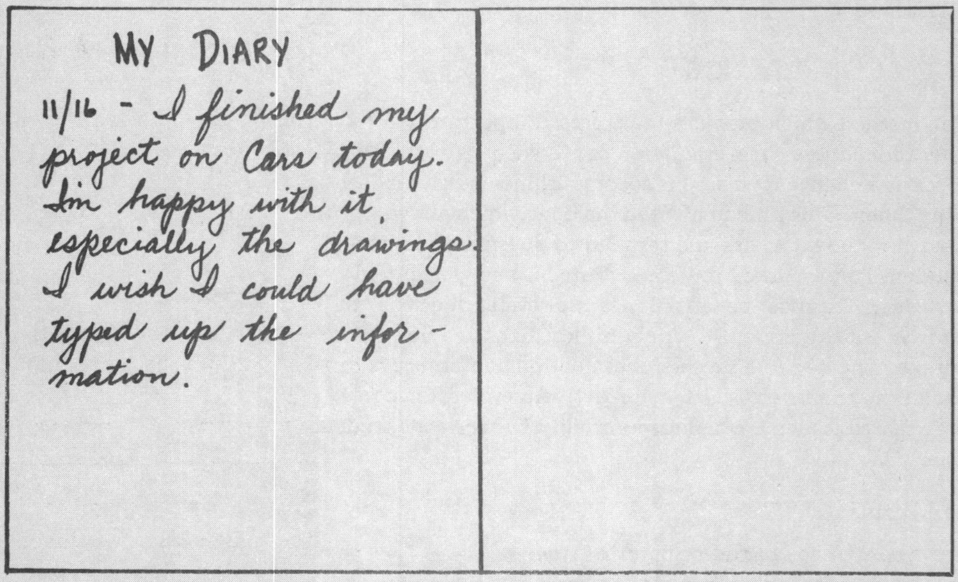

_____
_____
_____
_____
_____

MY DIARY

11/16 – I finished my project on cars today. I'm happy with it, especially the drawings. I wish I could have typed up the information.

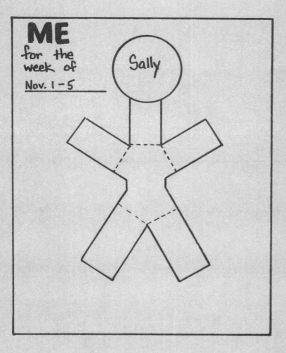

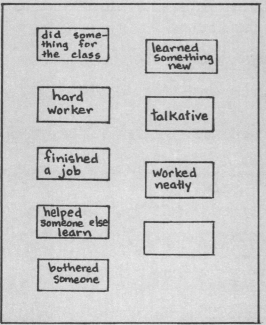

Me

The child draws his face onto the figure. At the close of each school week, he selects the characteristic which best describes him for that week. He cuts and pastes this onto the stick figure. The completed figure provides an accounting of the child's feeling about himself or his work.

Taking a Look at Myself

Effective with older children, this worksheet helps to differentiate the types of goals students can have as they work in the classroom. These goals can be related to a particular learning activity or to a given period of time within the school week. This type of device encourages a student to be responsible for his own learning and behavior.

Continuum

This instrument presents students with examples of behavior. Each behavior is shown with its opposite. Students are to place a mark on the continuum to indicate what they feel their behavior is most like. This can be filled out before and after a given period. In this way the student can compare how he expects to behave with his actual behavior.

Profile

Each child makes a profile of himself. In an individual conference with the teacher, learning or behavioral goals are set for the student. He records these on his profile. After a designated period of time, the student also records his accomplishments.

Look at Me!

I am...

a noisy worker———|———|———|———a quiet worker

a neat worker———|———|———|———a messy worker

able to work by———|———|———|———always asking
myself   for help

usually able to———|———|———|———usually can't
finish my work   finish my
                                                                    work

THIS IS _John W._

MY GOALS: I want to experiment to see which kind of soil grows the best plants.
I want to learn to play the autoharp.
I want to do better at not bothering others when they're working.
MY RECENT ACCOMPLISHMENTS:
I finished my seed-sprouting experiments.
I've really improved my cursive writing.
I learned to multiply and divide 2-place numbers.
I haven't been in a fight for 1 month.
DATE: Dec. 1

Worksheets

CONTENTS

BE A GOOD GARDENER

Grow the flowers in ABC order in the flower pot.

Show how an animal looks or acts in each setting.

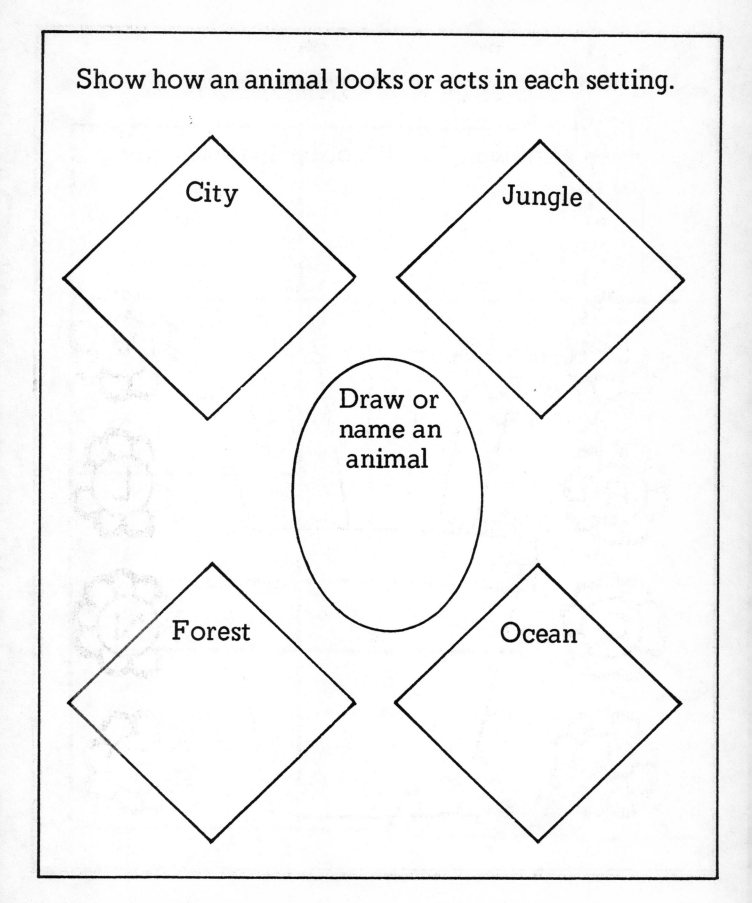

City

Jungle

Draw or
name an
animal

Forest

Ocean

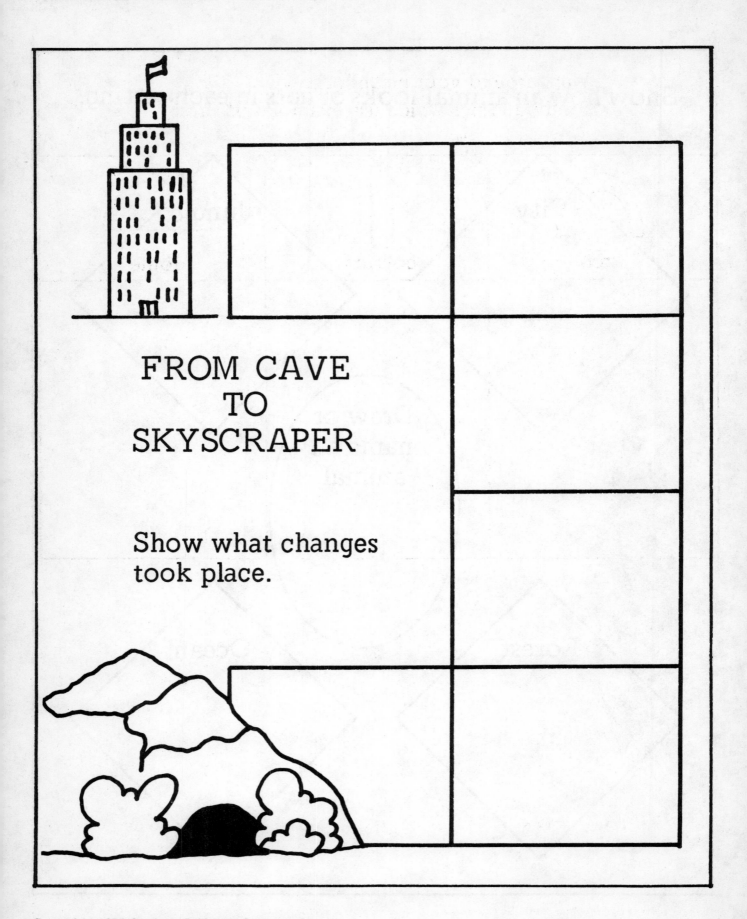

FROM CAVE
TO
SKYSCRAPER

Show what changes
took place.

Walk around your neighborhood.
Find buildings which use examples of these:

 arch	 column	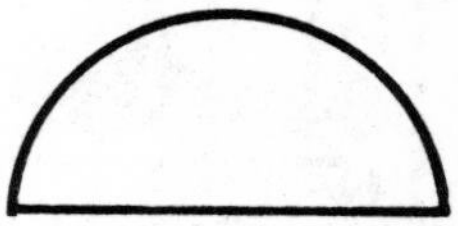 dome

Choose a painting in one of these styles. Draw it in its correct frame. Change it to show how it would look in one or both of the other styles.

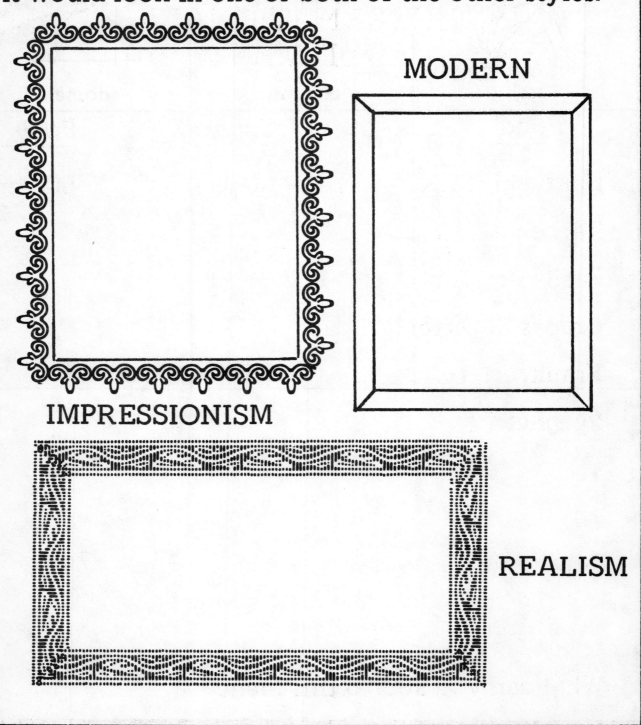

MODERN

IMPRESSIONISM

REALISM

INTERNATIONAL FOOD MENU

Food	Country	Price
Sukiyaki	Japan	50 yen
Tacos		
Paella		
Crepes Suzette		
Frankfurters		
Spaghetti		

What can you add to this menu?

What foods are made in these ways?

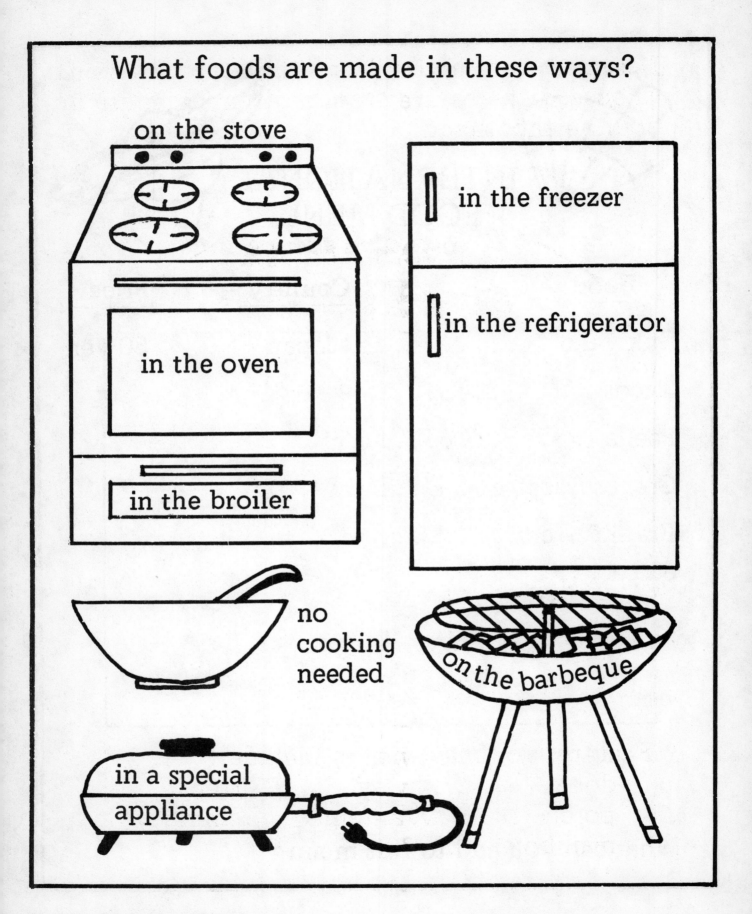

on the stove

in the freezer

in the oven

in the refrigerator

in the broiler

no cooking needed

on the barbeque

in a special appliance

Design a new house from those around you. Choose each feature from a different house in your neighborhood.

Design a Home

Features you may wish to include:

door	walkway	steps
porch	T.V. antenna	chimney
mail box	and ? ? ?	

ALIKE 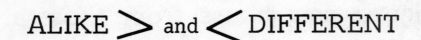 and DIFFERENT

Choose 6 houses on a block. Use words or drawings to compare a feature of the houses, such as T.V. antennas, doors, windows or shrubbery. Look for things that are alike and different.

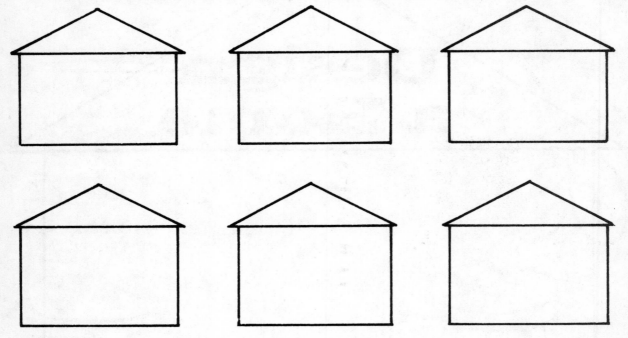

Color in the ingredients you would add to a fairy tale.

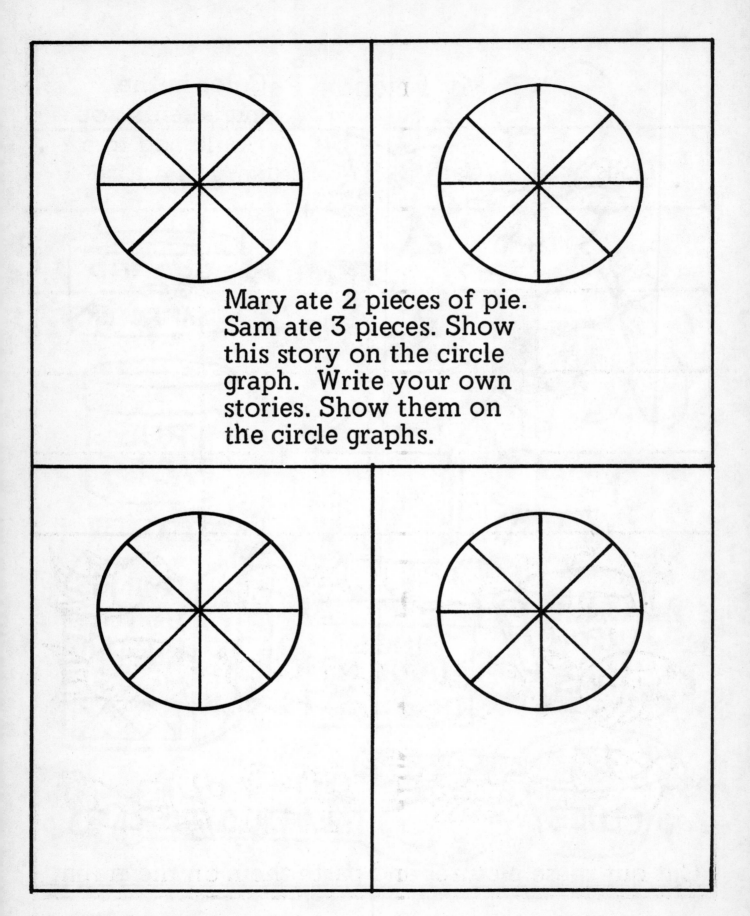

Mary ate 2 pieces of pie. Sam ate 3 pieces. Show this story on the circle graph. Write your own stories. Show them on the circle graphs.

My Friends' Pets

Dogs	Cats	Birds	Fish

Cut out these pictures and paste them on the graph.

TRACE–PRACTICE–PERFECT

1. Choose a letter to practice.
2. Have the teacher write it for you.
3. Trace the letter as many times as you need to.

f   *f f f*

k

h

Trace   Practice   Write your
perfect letter

Practice: your name
or
a word
or
a letter

Make it into a cartoon character.

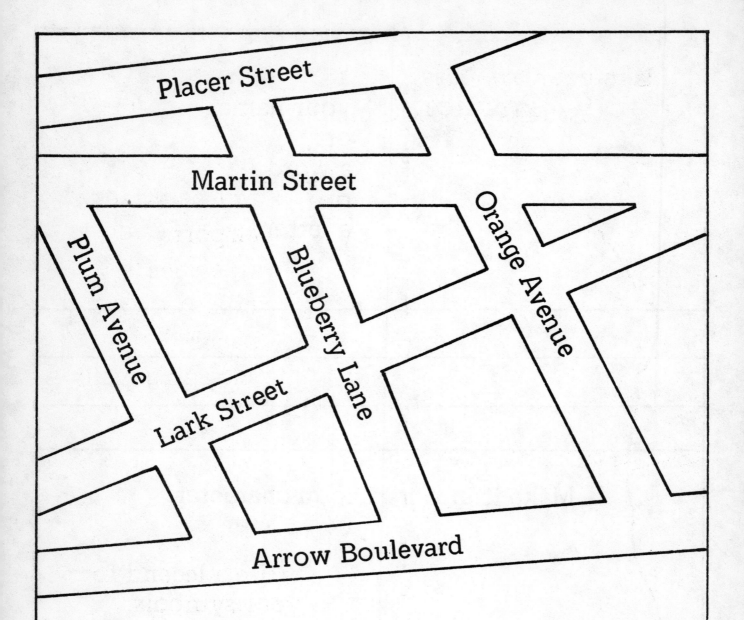

Map a route for an underground transit system using these streets.

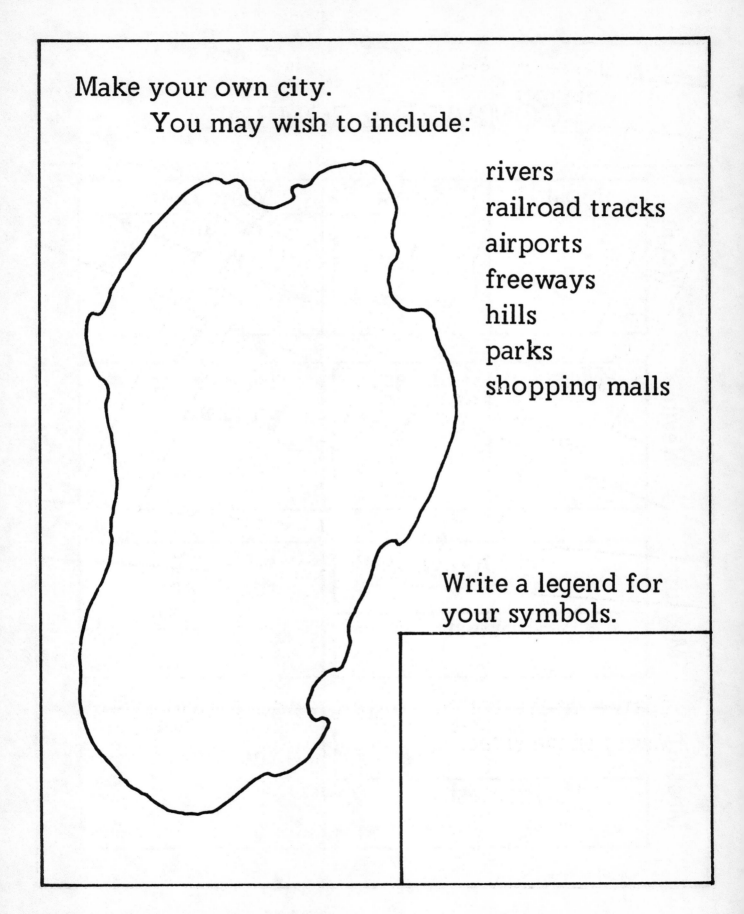

Make your own city.
   You may wish to include:

rivers
railroad tracks
airports
freeways
hills
parks
shopping malls

Write a legend for
your symbols.

COMPARE & COMBINE

Weigh	Most	Least	Make them the same

Weigh	Most	Least	Make them the same

Measure	Longest	Make them the same
	Shortest	

Measure	Longest	Make them the same
	Shortest	

FIND MACHINES THAT DO THE SAME KIND OF WORK AS THE TOOL

(For example, a screwdriver turns; what machines turn?)
Cut out or draw pictures to show them.

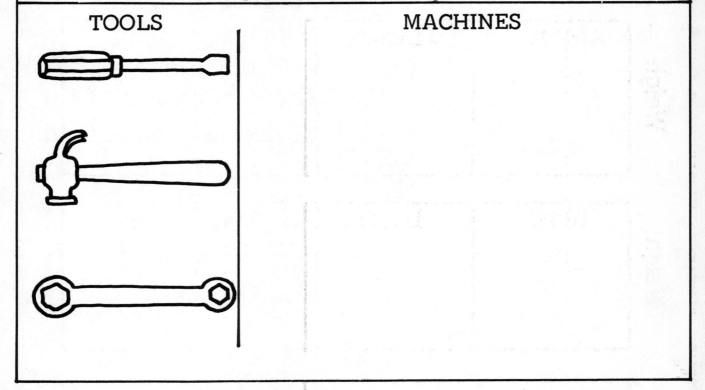

TOOLS	MACHINES

CRIME DETECTION LAB

How were the mysteries or crimes solved in the books you've read?

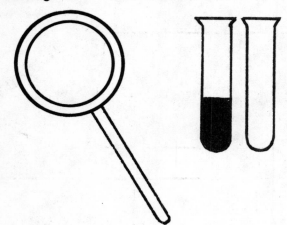

Draw examples of the devices that were used.

WALK THE MYSTERY TRAIL

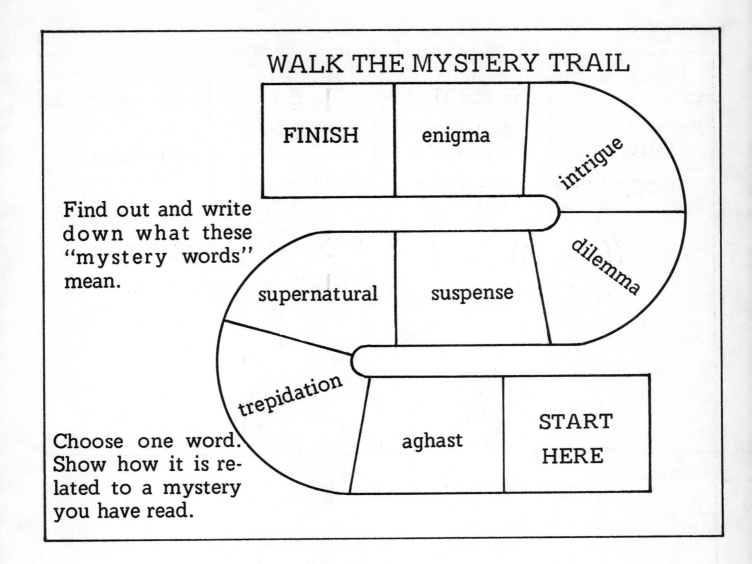

FINISH

enigma

intrigue

dilemma

Find out and write down what these "mystery words" mean.

supernatural

suspense

trepidation

Choose one word. Show how it is related to a mystery you have read.

aghast

START HERE

Take a survey of people's favorite songs.
What conclusions can you make based on your survey?

Favorite Song	Age of Person Surveyed	Occupation	Average time spent listening to radio per day

Conclusions:

*Make up another music survey.

Listen to 10 records at home or at school.
Write the song titles on one of the record categories below.

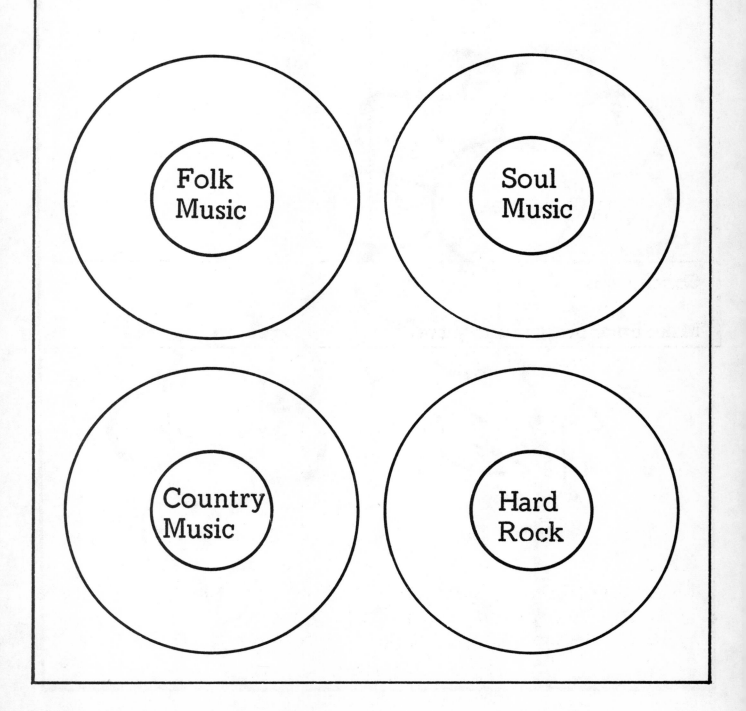

Fill the garden with synonym flowers.
How many can you grow?

Create the course that finishes the story by writing a part of it on each rocket.

Problem: Two space vehicles from different countries are on a "crash" course in space.

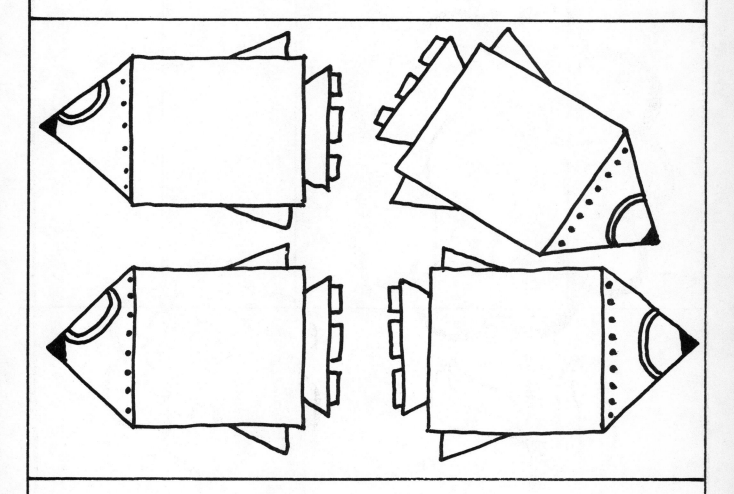

Solution: The Interplanetary Traffic Control Agency felt satisfied with their decision.

MAKE A SEQUENCE PUZZLE

Draw the main parts of your favorite story in the sections below. Paste this page on cardboard. Cut the sections apart to make a puzzle for others to do. Don't forget to put the answers on the back.

Sub Set Insects

Use the set members on the bodies to write subsets on the insects' legs.

Cut and paste the number that matches each set.

N { 🍎 🍌 🍐 } = ☐

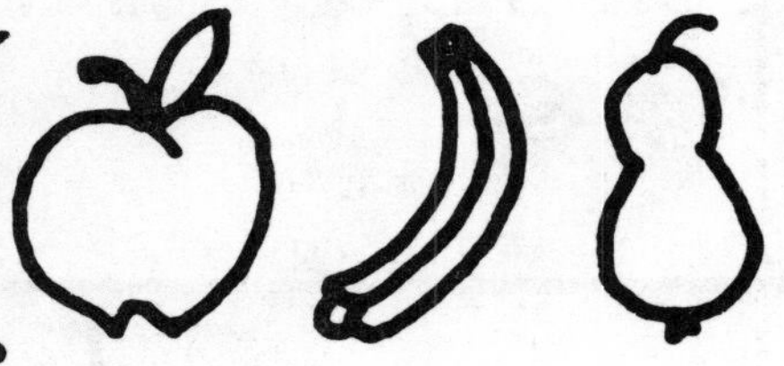

N { 🥛 ⊙ 🏺 🥄🍴 } = ☐

N { ▱ ▱ } = ☐

N { } = ☐

N { ⚾ ▪ ◇ ○ △ ▯ } = ☐

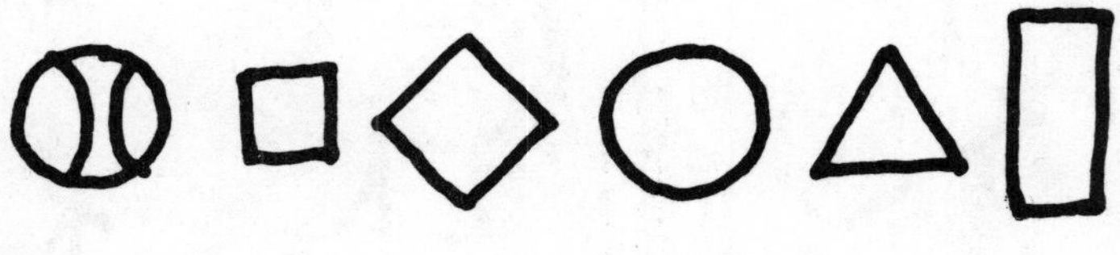

4	6	1	3	0	5	2

Sports using a ball

Sports played inside a building

Sports using a stick or racket

Sports using a wall, backboard or net

What do you know about these sports?

Use an encyclopedia or other books to see if you can find out more.

Sport	Country	Equipment	Number of Players	Playing Area
La Crosse				
Soccer				
Jai Alai				
Rugby				
Polo				

READ A
TALL
TALE

Write the TALL happenings from a TALL TALE
on each tree trunk.

DOES THE COMMERCIAL SELL?

Product: _____

Who are they trying to sell to? _____

_____

Do you think it's a good product? _____

Why? _____

_____

Would you buy it? _____

Elements of the commercial

_____ Musical jingle   _____ Slogan

_____ Background music   _____ Humor

_____ Well-known personality

_____ Factual information

_____ Other

Design your own commercial here.

Survey people to find out if they like your commercial.